THE EASY
Low-Sodium
Diet Plan
& COOKBOOK

English Cucumber Salad p.97

THE EASY
Low-Sodium
Diet Plan
& COOKBOOK

Quick-Fix & Slow Cooker Meals
to Start (& Stick to) a Low-Salt Diet

Christopher Lower

For my best friend, teammate, and true Wonder Woman with moxie; to my three Wonderkids, whose culinary flexibility and patience, love, and artwork keep me strong; and the countless extended neighborhood and church families who embraced our family as their own.

CONTENTS

INTRODUCTION

"The secret of change is to focus all of your energy not on fighting the old, but on building the new." – Socrates

Introducing a guide to changing your diet with a quote from a philosopher sentenced to death by hemlock poisoning may be slightly odd, but Socrates made a good point: You and I have been "sentenced" to giving up the eating habits we enjoy because they are ultimately killing us. I guarantee that it's not by fighting our old habits that we create a new rewarding and delicious culinary lifestyle, but by making small, easy changes over time.

What makes me such an expert? In 2002, I caught a virus while traveling for business and wound up with an infection that settled into the enzymes in the fluid that surrounds my heart, causing the heart muscle tissue to inflame and enlarge. That was the beginning of my heart-health journey, which included tons of medications, a pacemaker, defibrillator, an LVAD (Left Ventricular Assist Device), the transplant list, and, in May 2014, a heart transplant.

As a 6'2" former football player, I hated diets—I figured starting one meant ending it someday. To experience true success, I had to change my lifestyle. I hated the denial aspect of diets; I needed to be able to eat the foods I wanted but find a way to make them healthy. I needed to lose the salt without sacrificing taste. It helps that I have an incredible wife and three wonderful children who have been my reason for being and fighting through all of these health challenges. They have also been my co-conspirators, sous chefs, tasters, and critics in my efforts to make our family's meals healthier and tastier, too.

This book is designed to help my fellow sojourners transition to a low- or no-sodium lifestyle. I provide recipes, tips, tricks, tools, and products that fit into this new way of living. To make it even easier to transition into a healthier way of eating, each recipe comes complete with its own nutritional label as a guideline. I take into consideration various health conditions that can be positively affected by maintaining a low-sodium diet, including hypertension, cardiac disease, and Menière's Disease, and I'll pay special attention to how potassium affects low-sodium diets.

I've also included unique menu-specific plans and recipes differentiating between hypertension and cardiac disease sufferers. Don't worry if you're not a terrific chef—each section includes super-simple slow-cooker recipes in which you chop, add to the pot, and cover—and dinner is done when you get home from work!

I don't include anything in this book if I haven't personally tried it. I am on a lifelong journey to find the best low- and no-sodium solutions, and am excited to share the past 15 years of my personal experience with you. Let's get started.

PART

1

LOW SODIUM AND YOU

1

WHERE DIET AND HEALTH INTERSECT

If you are reading this, you've probably been told that, for health reasons, you need to reduce the amount of sodium in your diet. Maybe you have been diagnosed with one of the many conditions where you would benefit from a low-sodium diet, such as high blood pressure, heart disease, kidney disease, liver disease, Menière's disease, or another condition.

You may have been surprised by your diagnosis, and you may still be in shock or denial, but now you are asking yourself: How do I start a low-sodium diet? My own journey to a low-sodium diet began with cardiac disease and high blood pressure, so I understand what you are going through and I'm here to help.

Sodium is a major contributor to high blood pressure, and many Americans unwittingly consume up to 20 times more sodium than their body needs each day. In this chapter, we will examine sodium, the unexpected places where it is found in our diets, and how to limit sodium consumption in an effort to live longer, healthier lives.

About Sodium

Sodium chloride (NaCL), or salt, is an electrolyte (an electrically conducting solution when dissolved in water) that is an essential part of our physical makeup, allowing our bodies to function optimally. Sodium balances the body's fluid levels, allows for the transmission of signals from nerves, aids our muscles in movement, and helps with digestion.

However, like all the other electrolytes in our bodies (potassium, calcium, magnesium, bicarbonate, chloride, and hydrogen phosphate), salt must be maintained within a certain healthy level. Extremely low sodium is as dangerous as extremely high sodium. If your body has extremely low sodium, your heart may not generate the electricity needed to make it beat, or it may cause your heart to go into a rapid heartbeat that could be dangerous. High sodium, over time, leads to hypertension, which can damage the veins, arteries, kidneys, and heart. That can lead to further heart disease. Therefore, it's important to consult your physician to determine the proper salt balance for you.

Sodium makes our bodies draw extra water into our blood vessels and increases the blood volume in our arteries and veins, which can cause high blood pressure. Heart.org likens it to "turning up the supply in a garden hose." If a high level of sodium continues to remain in the blood stream, our blood vessels can become permanently stretched and strained. It is this damage, weakness, and inflexibility (you may have heard the phrase "hardening of the arteries") that leads to heart attacks later in life.

If your doctor has determined that you should begin controlling your sodium levels, he or she more than likely also gave you a daily limit of grams or milligrams of sodium. If not, ask your practitioner for a specific number to aim for before beginning a low-sodium diet.

The United States Department of Agriculture (USDA) recommends 2,300 milligrams (mg) of sodium per day for a healthy person without high blood pressure or heart disease. The American Heart Association (AHA) recommends 1,500 mg per day. Recently, the Mayo Clinic recommended

THE TRUTH ABOUT SEA SALT AND SALT REPLACEMENTS

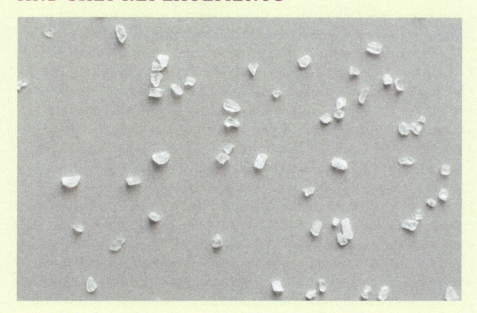

Salt is salt is salt. At its molecular core, it is all Sodium Chloride (NaCl). Sea salt may have a better taste or trace minerals that may be good for you, but it is still salt. It comes with fancy names on packages: Fleur de Sel, Celtic Gray, Himalayan, Pink Hawaiian, and so on, but it is still detrimental to your health in quantities above 1,500 mg a day.

Most salt replacements use potassium chloride. **Potassium chloride must be avoided by heart, liver, and kidney patients**, as it interacts negatively with most of the medicines used to treat those conditions (such as aspirin, Coumadin, Lasix [furosemide, metoprolol], Plavix, antirejection medications [Prograf, tacrolimus, sirolimus, mycophenolate], vitamin B_{12}, and Lantus). For those who have had heart transplants, like me, and regularly take those medications, it's especially challenging to make sure that any low-sodium items used are truly low in sodium *and* do not use potassium chloride as a replacement for salt.

1,500 mg of sodium per day for all Americans aged 51 and above. (The disparity between the USDA and AHA and Mayo Clinic is because the USDA has not reviewed their recommendations recently, whereas the other two organizations review medical research and findings regularly.) The problem is, most Americans consume 3,000 to 6,000 mg of sodium on a daily basis.

You may think: *Okay, 1,500 mg or less a day doesn't sound too bad. I can do that.* But what does that really look like? It's surprising how little 1,500 mg of sodium actually amounts to: It is equal to ¾ teaspoon of salt. You read that correctly—LESS than ONE teaspoon. *But I behave; I rarely use the salt shaker to add extra salt on my food!* Unfortunately, most of the sodium we consume comes from the processed foods we eat. Sodium is everywhere—in baked goods, cheeses, deli meats, sauces—almost everything we purchase.

But never fear! It is possible to enjoy your food on 1,500 mg of sodium per day. By using this book as a guide to create a healthy low-sodium lifestyle, you can start taking action immediately to lower your risk—or the risk of someone you love—of having a first (or subsequent) heart attack(s). Together, we will discover some new skills to succeed at living a low-sodium life. Learning how to effectively read and understand food labels, and becoming accustomed to cooking healthy food at home will be the two most beneficial skills you can acquire and improve upon.

Understanding Your Diagnosis: High Blood Pressure

Unless your doctor has already diagnosed you with high blood pressure, you may not have a clear idea of what constitutes "good" blood pressure versus "bad." Simply put, having high blood pressure means that your heart has to work harder to pump blood through your body, and this extra work puts excess pressure on your arteries, which creates tension that makes it that much harder for your heart to do its job.

When you visit your doctor's office for a blood pressure reading, the doctor logs two numbers:

- **Systolic** (the top/"over" number) indicates how much pressure your blood is exerting against your artery walls when the heart beats.
- **Diastolic** (the lower number) indicates how much pressure your blood is exerting against your artery walls while the heart is at rest between beats.

While having a higher than normal reading for either number isn't ideal (see the following chart for your target blood pressure range), it is usually the top, or systolic number that is considered more important. The latest research shows that the systolic blood pressure gives the best indication of your risk of having a stroke or heart attack.

What causes high blood pressure? Essential (primary) hypertension has no known cause. It gradually develops over time. Secondary hypertension is caused by other conditions such as kidney disease, some birth control pills, sleep apnea, and more.

The scariest part about high blood pressure is that while it can do so much damage, it typically has no signs or symptoms—one out of every five people

BLOOD PRESSURE CATEGORY	SYSTOLIC MM HG (UPPER #)		DIASTOLIC MM HG (LOWER #)	
Normal	less than 120	and	less than 80	★
Prehypertension	120 – 139	or	80 – 89	
High Blood Pressure (Hypertension) Stage 1	140 – 159	or	90 – 99	
High Blood Pressure (Hypertension) Stage 2	160 or higher	or	100 or higher	
Hypertensive Crisis (Emergency care needed)	Higher than 180	or	Higher than 110	!

Source: http://www.heart.org/HEARTORG/Conditions/HighBloodPressure/UnderstandSymptomsRisks/Why-High-Blood-Pressure-is-a-Silent-Killer_UCM_002053_Article.jsp#.WLXcPI-cFPY with high blood pressure don't even know they have it. The only way to know whether you're in the normal range or have high blood pressure is to get checked regularly.

There is no cure for high blood pressure, but it can be controlled. You must consistently monitor your blood pressure and manage it through sensible lifestyle changes such as a low sodium diet, regular exercise, and ceasing smoking. (Always consult your doctor before beginning a lifestyle change, and to determine your optimal blood pressure numbers.)

Improving your diet and maintaining your sodium can provide noticeable health benefits in a short time. You should have less water retention and bloating as you reduce the levels of sodium you intake. Carrying less water weight means the heart doesn't have to work as hard to push the blood through your body. If you tend to carry water weight in your abdomen, then less water retention in that area means that the weight of that water isn't impairing your lungs and breathing. It will also reduce the workload of the kidneys, and improved blood flow to the kidneys can allow for even less water retention.

Understanding Your Diagnosis: Heart Disease

Heart disease is the leading cause of death for both men and women in the United States. It can occur at any age, however. In the United States, four out of five people who die from coronary heart disease are aged 65 or older.

According to the National Institute of Health (NIH), "Coronary heart disease—often simply called heart disease—is the main form of heart disease. It is a disorder of the blood vessels of the heart that can lead to heart attack. A heart attack happens when an artery becomes blocked, preventing oxygen and nutrients from getting to the heart. Heart disease is one of several cardiovascular diseases, which are diseases of the heart and blood vessel system. Other cardiovascular diseases include stroke, high blood pressure, angina (chest pain), and rheumatic heart disease."

Sadly, due to the lack of attention some people place on the health of their hearts, many people are diagnosed only after they have experienced a major heart episode, such as a heart attack or stroke. Your primary doctor diagnoses coronary heart disease (CHD) based on your medical and family histories, your risk factors, a physical exam, and the results from tests and procedures. If your primary doctor does not have experience, or if your case is serious, you may be referred to a cardiologist.

There are several tests to determine your risk, whether or not you have CHD, and if you do, at what stage of CHD you are currently at. Some of the tests are (for more in-depth descriptions, visit the National Institutes of Health online):

EKG (Electrocardiogram). An EKG detects and records the heart's electrical activity.

Stress Testing. During stress testing, you exercise to make your heart work hard and beat fast while heart tests are done.

Echocardiography. Echocardiography (or echo) uses sound waves to create a moving picture of your heart. The test provides information about the size and shape of your heart and how well your heart chambers and valves are working.

Chest X-ray. A chest X-ray can reveal signs of heart failure, as well as lung disorders and other causes of symptoms not related to CHD.

Blood Tests. Blood tests check the levels of certain fats, cholesterol, sugar, and proteins in your blood. Abnormal levels may be a sign that you're at risk. Blood tests also help detect anemia, a risk factor for CHD.

Coronary Angiography and Cardiac Catheterization. Your doctor may recommend coronary angiography if other tests or factors suggest you have CHD. This test uses dye and special X-rays to look inside your coronary arteries.

What are the risk factors for heart disease? The following risk factors don't automatically mean you have CHD, but they all contribute to the probability you may contract CHD without changing your habits and lifestyle:

- High blood pressure
- High blood cholesterol
- Diabetes and prediabetes
- Smoking
- Being overweight or obese
- Being physically inactive
- Having a family history of early heart disease
- Having a history of preeclampsia during pregnancy
- Unhealthy diet
- Age (50 or older for men and women. Those of African-American descent have even greater risk factors)

Cardiovascular disease symptoms may be different for men and women. For instance, men are more likely to have chest pain; women are more likely to have symptoms such as shortness of breath, nausea, and extreme fatigue.

Symptoms for men and women can include:

- Chest pain (angina)
- Shortness of breath
- Pain, numbness, weakness, or coldness in your legs or arms if the blood vessels in those parts of your body are narrowed
- Pain in the neck, jaw, throat, upper abdomen, or back
- Fluttering in your chest
- Racing heartbeat (tachycardia)
- Slow heartbeat (bradycardia)
- Chest pain or discomfort
- Lightheadedness
- Dizziness
- Fainting (syncope) or near fainting
- Breathlessness with exertion or at rest
- Swelling of the legs, ankles, and feet
- Fatigue

Reducing sodium and improving your diet can ease your symptoms as they do for high blood pressure sufferers. You should see less water retention and bloating as you reduce the levels of sodium, which allows your heart to not work as hard.

MENIÈRE'S DISEASE

In the late 1800s at the Institute for Deaf-Mutes, French physician Prosper Menière concentrated his studies on a condition that combined hearing loss, tinnitus (or "ringing in the ear"), and vertigo (or dizziness), which was named in his honor as "Menière's Disease."

While an exact cause for Menière's disease hasn't been specifically determined, one common result of the unnerving disorder is an accumulation of fluid in the inner ear.

Contributing factors to the disease could be heredity, allergies, head trauma, migraines, the result of an infection, or a combination of these factors.

As in all other parts of the human body, salt can also cause fluid accumulation in the inner ear. By limiting sodium intake and spacing intake throughout the day, you can help your body manage and process sodium more effectively. (Although the meal plans in the book don't explicitly address Menière's Disease, they can still be followed to help ease symptoms.)

While there is no cure for Menière's Disease, limiting salt, not smoking, avoiding caffeine and alcohol, and reducing stress have all been shown to help cope with and reduce attacks.

If symptoms are more severe, medications to quell the dizziness and shorten the length of attacks are available, as are antibiotic or corticosteroid injections into the middle ear to lessen vertigo.

Some patients find value in having short bursts of air delivered through an "air pulse generator" (a tube placed in the ear drum), an endolymphatic shunt (or tube) implanted to drain fluid from the ear, or other more in-depth inner ear surgeries depending on the severity of the patient's symptoms.

If you think that you may have Menière's Disease, please check with your doctor or physician immediately, who can provide additional information and help you manage your condition.

CONSIDERING POTASSIUM

Potassium helps counteract the effects of sodium—it relaxes blood vessels, thus lowering blood pressure, and helps remove sodium through the urine.

Most Americans do not reach the recommended daily allowance, but before going overboard, it's important to note that too much potassium can damage the kidneys.

To boost potassium in your diet, add foods such as bananas, beans, sweet potatoes, and tomatoes. Proponents of the National Institutes of Health DASH (Dietary Approaches to Stop Hypertension) Diet (dashdiet.org) developed a low-sodium diet high in fruits and vegetables, lean meats, low-fat and nonfat dairy, and whole grains—all foods naturally high in potassium.

Some medications, such as diuretics in the aldactone family, preserve levels of potassium. Do not increase potassium in your diet if you are on these medications. Avoid foods that have ingredients labeled potassium or K, KCl, or K+—the chemical symbols for potassium and related compounds.

Health Harvard offers these additional helpful tips if you are looking to lower the amount of potassium in your diet:

- Soak or boil vegetables and fruits to leach out some potassium.
- Avoid canned, salted, pickled, corned, spiced, and smoked meat and fish.
- Avoid imitation meat products containing soy or vegetable protein.
- Limit high-potassium fruits such as bananas, citrus fruits, and avocados.
- Avoid baked potatoes and baked acorn and butternut squash.
- Avoid all types of peas and beans, which are naturally high in potassium.

Some salt substitutes will also be very high in potassium, so be sure to carefully check the label before you purchase or liberally apply to your food.

Source: www.health.harvard.edu/heart-health/heart-failure-and-potassium

The Challenge and the Solution

When adopting a low-sodium diet, the USDA goal is to consume less than 2,300 mg of sodium a day. For the plan in this book, we use the Mayo Clinic's goal of 1,500 mg a day. Sodium is absolutely everywhere, even in places you think it can't possibly be, such as breakfast cereal, breads, and "all natural" frozen chicken: the birds (even organically raised fliers) are pumped full of salt water prior to freezing to enhance appearance and—surprise— taste. So, really, it's difficult to ditch salt when it imparts a lot of the flavor we're used to.

One of the tools I found most helpful was learning to substitute spices for salt. I live in Minnesota, and here we often joke about how black pepper is considered a "spice." I promise we will venture beyond black pepper and Mrs. Dash in the spice department.

If there are other vitamins or minerals that can interfere with your health, we will do our best to address them; however, and I simply cannot stress this enough: This book is not intended to be a substitute for a medical diagnosis. Before starting any diet or medical plan, please consult your doctor or physician.

This book will help you relearn to cook, guide you in finding substitutions (including kitchen staples and condiments), and help you enjoy your way to a low-sodium diet.

2

IN THE KITCHEN

This book is a partnership in wellness. I promise not to send you in search of hard-to-find ingredients, or suggest you take on recipes that are too difficult to prepare in an average kitchen, using average ingredients and equipment. In return, I hope you'll give this new diet a truly genuine try, and trust me when I say that the recipes in the book are delicious enough for my family—who don't have to decrease their salt intake.

In this chapter we'll talk about cleaning out your kitchen of foods that hinder your health and incorporating foods that help it. What equipment will you need? And is changing your lifestyle going to break the budget? Read on for more.

Remember, while going low-sodium can be called a diet, it is more than just "a diet." It is a lifestyle change; it has to be. You can't change your eating habits for three months, then go back to eating an entire take-out pizza three days a week with a bag of potato chips on the side and expect that your heart is going to stay healthy. You only get one heart.

Eating Well to Live Well

Remember back in the beginning of the book where I promised to prove to you that by not fighting our old habits, but by making small and easy changes over time, we can create a new lifestyle that will be just as rewarding and equally delicious? Read on, and I'll deliver on that promise.

Getting Rid of the Bad Stuff

The first small step is doing a kitchen inventory. That means going through your entire kitchen and getting rid of all foods that no longer fit into your new low-sodium lifestyle. If there are unopened containers of food that you can't use anymore, consider donating them to a food bank or giving them away to family and friends. I suggest getting rid of open containers of high-sodium condiments such as soy sauce, ketchup, and taco seasonings, but if members of your household still use them and you trust yourself to self-police, you can keep them in the house for others to use until they are done. Do not repurchase.

MANAGING YOUR BUDGET

Here are a few tips for reducing costs and added convenience:

1. Plan meals and make lists. This allows you to plan ahead and avoid extraneous purchases when shopping.
2. Use coupon apps. Many retailers and manufacturers put their coupons online.
3. Comparison shop online. Make sure you find the best sources to get what you need at the best prices.
4. Buy bulk of common goods that you use weekly. Purchasing foods like rice, beans, condiments, no-salt-added canned goods, and spices in bulk can be a real money saver.
5. Visit discount store chains for great prices. Think dollar stores, Aldi's, Trader Joe's, Big Lots, etc.

Here's a quick look at the top ten culprits with the highest sodium in most kitchens:

- Deli meat
- Breakfast cereal
- Canned soup
- Flavor packets and condiments
- Spaghetti sauce
- Bread and tortillas
- Dairy products
- Canned meat and seafood
- Frozen meals

In general, anything with 140 mg of sodium per serving is considered low-sodium and can remain as a staple. Those foodstuffs with 400 mg of sodium or more per serving are high-sodium and can no longer remain in your daily diet. Items in between 140 mg and 400 mg are not low-sodium items and should be used rarely if you decide to keep them in your pantry.

Rebuild and Regroup: Updating Pantry Staples

Now that you've taken your pantry apart, it's time to replace sodium-rich items with low-sodium items.

The best way to eat healthier is to eat fresh! Eating seasonally is generally going to be easier on the wallet, as well as being definitely delicious, and—since you'll be making your own food at home—you can control the flavor and the salt.

For a comprehensive list of seasonal fruits and vegetables, visit Fruits & Veggies—More Matters. And remember, you can enjoy the taste of any fruit or vegetable year-round by using fresh, frozen, no-sodium canned, dried, or 100 percent juice. Shopping and eating seasonally (or by using the equivalent frozen version) will help ensure that your diet stays varied and interesting and that you never run out of ideas for recipes and new things to try with your new lifestyle.

When restocking your low- and no-sodium pantry with healthy options, focus on the following items:

- No-salt-added stocks and broths for making homemade soups and boosting flavor in other homemade dishes including rice, potatoes, and pastas
- Dry rice, potatoes, and pastas
- Low- or no-sodium mustards—stone-ground are usually the lowest in sodium

- Low- or no-sodium salsa
- Low- or no-sodium hot sauces add zing and flavor
- Multiple vinegars—malt, white wine, red wine, cider, rice wine, and regular and white balsamic add fantastic bright and varied flavors and have the added benefit of a low glycemic index
- Sodium- and potassium-free baking soda and powder
- Spice blends from brands such as McCormick's, Dak's, Mrs. Dash, and Weber for blends like blackened seasoning, Cajun, BBQ, Asian, etc.
- Salt-free liquid smoke
- Lemons and limes

As with all other foods, keep in mind that certain fruits and vegetables have a high natural potassium content that may affect your health. Vegetables with naturally high potassium include squash, oranges, broccoli, cantaloupe, raisins, kale, grapes, sweet potatoes, beans, broccoli, and bananas. According to *Diet & Fitness Today*, herbs high in potassium include chervil, coriander, parsley, basil, dill weed, tarragon, turmeric, paprika, red and cayenne pepper, spearmint, and chili powder.

A FEW GOOD BRANDS

In addition to the fresh meats, fruits, and veggies you're going to be incorporating in your diet, here are a few of my hacking salt "must-haves" for any low-sodium pantry (presented in no particular order):

- Hormel breast of chicken in water, no salt added, has 70 mg sodium per 2-ounce serving
- Green Giant Niblets sweet corn, no salt added, has 10 mg sodium in 1/3 cup
- B&G Crunchy Kosher Dill Chips, unsalted, has 0 mg sodium in a 1-ounce serving
- Del Monte fresh-cut French-style green beans, no salt added, has 10 mg sodium in 1/2 cup
- Hunt's tomato products, no salt added. The paste has 30 mg sodium in 2 tablespoons, the sauce has 20 mg sodium in 1/4 cup, and the stewed tomatoes have 30 mg sodium in 1/2 cup
- Health Valley Organic soup, no salt added. The tomato soup has 35 mg sodium in 1 cup, and the lentil soup has 25 mg sodium in 1 cup

- Eden Organic beans, no salt added. The pinto beans have 15 mg sodium in ½ cup, the kidney beans have 15 mg sodium in ½ cup, and the garbanzo beans have 3 mg sodium in ½ cup
- Other salt-free spices and marinades that you discover and find that you like

For more nutritional information on these must-haves and to see more low-sodium options, check out www.bhg.com/recipes/healthy/low-sodium /best-low-sodium-pantry-picks/. And remember to check for hidden potassium chloride in all your seasoning choices.

Some Cooking Rules

In general, reducing sodium in your home meals is pretty simple. A few replacements here and there and you won't know the difference. Dietitian Toby Amidor at Food Network's *Healthy Eats* blog has a great listing of her top simple ways to reduce sodium in our home meals. The following are some tips that I think work well with our meal plans.

Replace canned veggies with fresh or frozen. Toby reminds us that ½ cup of canned vegetables contains approximately 15 percent of daily sodium requirements.

Make your own potato chips. If you have a dehydrator, make your own veggie chips. It's fast and simple.

Make your own condiment substitutes. We will be providing lots of recipes for low-sodium ketchups, broths, and sauces, but also try mixing different vinegars, spices, and juices for your salad dressings.

Use less canned spaghetti sauce. Jarred spaghetti sauce has a lot of sodium. One cup typically has 50 percent of your daily sodium needs. Consider making your own no-salt version, plus make your own pesto.

Cook your own meals. Preprepared meals, whether frozen or at restaurants have way more salt than we need. Frozen entrées sometimes have up to 67 percent of daily sodium requirements and, as mentioned earlier, restaurant chefs do love their salt. By prepping and cooking your own simple meals, like the ones in this book, you know exactly what's in your food.

YOUR AMAZING SLOW COOKER

To prepare many of the recipes in this book, you'll need a slow cooker. Why? Because slow cookers make cooking incredibly easy, and your new lifestyle is all about easy. They generally involve only two steps: 1. Prepare and 2. Plug in. No need to sauté or braise anything.

For these recipes, you will use a 4-quart slow cooker. If you already own a slow cooker of a larger size, that's no problem—you can still use it for these recipes. If you need to purchase one, make sure the one you decide one that has a removable crock, so you can pop that part into the dishwasher after dinner. If you don't have a lift-out model, Crock-Pot liners—essentially heatproof large plastic bags that are used as cooking bags—are easy to find, then simply tossed away.

If buying a new Crock-Pot is not in your budget, check Craigslist, eBay, garage sales, or ask around. Oftentimes, people *have* Crock-Pots but aren't using them, and they sit gathering dust. Put that little guy to good use.

Rinse your canned beans. Or, better yet, use dried beans. But if you do use canned, rinsing that sugar-and-salt brine can reduce sodium content by 10 to 45 percent, depending on how well you rinse. Using dried beans leaves you with just the natural sodium content in the legume itself (if there was any at all). For example, a 3.5-ounce serving of boiled, dried red kidney beans contains 2 mg of sodium or less than 1 percent of the daily value. A drained, canned serving of red kidney beans has 231 mg of sodium, or slightly over 15 percent.

Understanding Nutrition Labels

As you begin a low-sodium diet, to keep your diet on track, it is vital to check the labels of every item you load into your shopping cart. Sodium counts are important, but it is even more important to check how many servings are in the package and the size of each serving. For example, the 10-ounce bag of Lay's classic potato chips has 10 servings—one serving is 1 ounce, which amounts to 15 chips. Each serving size has 170 mg salt. If you sit in front of the TV and absentmindedly go through the entire bag, you'll have blown past 1,500 mg of sodium in one sitting.

Most nutrition labels are on the back, bottom, or side of the packaging. Typically, specific nutrition information is not on the front, though the front is where you may find targeted marketing language that is worded to lure consumers into believing a product is low sodium.

The US Food and Drug Administration (FDA) and USDA both have strict guidelines in place that food manufacturers must follow if they want to label foods "healthy." According to government regulations and guidelines, food *cannot* be labeled as "healthy" if it has "more than 480 mg of sodium per labeled serving (for individual foods) or more than 600 mg of sodium per labeled serving for meals/main dishes."

Advertising and marketing language might sound healthy, but here is what some of those terms actually mean:

Sodium-Free Less than 5 mg of sodium per serving, and sodium chloride–free

Very Low Sodium 35 mg or less per serving

Low Sodium 140 mg or less per serving

Reduced (or Less) Sodium At least 25 percent less sodium per serving than the usual sodium level of a similar product

Light *(for sodium-reduced products)* If the food is categorized as low-calorie and low-fat and its sodium is reduced by at least 50 percent per serving than the usual sodium level for a similar product

Light in Sodium If sodium is reduced by at least 50 percent per serving than the usual sodium level for a similar product

In addition to looking for the sodium listing on the nutrition label, note that sodium also lurks under different names when used as a food additive, or in the preservation of processed, packaged, canned, jarred, or frozen foods.

Here are some of the more common forms of "indirect" sodium to look out for when reading labels:

- Sodium bicarbonate, or baking soda, sometimes just called "soda"
- Sodium nitrate
- Sodium citrate
- Sodium benzoate
- Monosodium glutamate (MSG)

Now, let's take a look at the back label, where you'll find serving sizes and amounts, calories, amounts of carbs, protein, fat, and sodium.

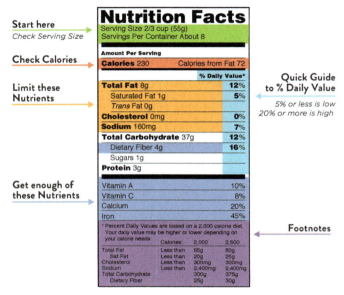

https://www.fda.gov/Food/GuidanceRegulation/GuidanceDocumentsRegulatoryInformation/LabelingNutrition/ucm385663.htm

Serving Size shows the amount of food represented by the nutritional elements listed. In our example, each service size is ½ cup. So within that one-half cup are all of the nutritional facts noted in the label, for example, there are 3 g of fat in the ½ cup serving size.

Servings Per Container tells you how many servings are in each package. In our example, there are 4 servings, each of ½ cup. Whenever consuming more than one serving, be sure to multiply the nutritional information amounts, so if we consume two servings, we also consume twice the amount of sodium, fats, carbs, and everything else listed on the label.

Calories are how a food's energy is measured. This serving has 90 calories.

Total Fat is the total amount of saturated, trans, polyunsaturated, and monounsaturated fats in one serving. Fats such as those found in Omega-3 fatty acids and some nuts are thought to be healthier for your heart, whereas saturated fats should be consumed in limited quantities and trans fats not at all, if your goal is to protect against heart disease.

Cholesterol is found in animal-based products. As with fats, the bottom line is that too much cholesterol can lead to heart disease.

Sodium shows us how much sodium is in each serving. In this example, there are 300 mg (13 percent daily value) sodium in one serving.

Total Carbohydrate is the total amount of starch, sugar, and fiber found in a single serving. Each of those subcategories is broken down on the label.

Protein helps build muscle and provides our muscles with energy. Some sources of protein, such as red meats and dairy products, can be high in cholesterol and fat. Choosing lean meats, fish, and low-fat or nut/plant milk products, as well as including plant-based proteins in your diet aid in maintaining a healthier lifestyle.

Vitamin A, Vitamin C, Iron, and Calcium are nutrients that are required to be listed on every food label. These are often nutrients that are scarce in our daily diets and should be watched.

Percent Daily Values are the percentages of nutrients in one serving of food. These are based upon the standards established for people who eat about 2,000 calories a day. Remember, not everyone needs that many calories each day, so you would have to calculate your daily values of a food based on your caloric needs.

Finally, you should always consult your physician before starting any diet. I got my information from my personal research and from my own physicians at the University of Minnesota Heart Clinic, but I am not an expert.

Low-Sodium Essential Equipment

In addition to the usual pots, pans, knives, whisks, and everything else in a conventional kitchen, there are a few essentials to get you going on your low-sodium lifestyle.

- A smartphone or computer to do research, access nutritional information, find new products, and so much more.

- A food thermometer, because food safety is a priority for those of us with suppressed immune systems. By measuring internal food temperature, you ensure that all food is cooked to perfection. Simple digital thermometers are available online or at a local store for less than $20. The chart below has basic guidelines, but visit www.fsis.usda.gov/ for more details on safe internal food temperatures.
- An indoor grill pan is a must for me and my no-salt lifestyle. With grilling and smoking, I add flavors that are "lost" otherwise when removing salt from my diet.
- A rice cooker, because all the different types of rice are great low sodium foods! Plus, you can make rice and vegetables by cooking the veggies alongside the rice in the rice cooker. When spices and herbs are added, they infuse flavor directly into the meal during the cooking period.

Food Temperature Chart

PRODUCT	MINIMUM INTERNAL TEMPERATURE & REST TIME
Beef, pork, veal & lamb Steaks, chops, roasts	145 °F (62.8 °C) and allow to rest for at least 3 minutes
Ground meats	160 °F (71.1 °C)
Ham, fresh or smoked (uncooked)	145 °F (62.8 °C) and allow to rest for at least 3 minutes
Fully cooked ham (to reheat)	Reheat cooked hams packaged in USDA-inspected plants to 140 °F (60 °C) and all others to 165 °F (73.9 °C).
All poultry (breasts, whole bird, legs, thighs, and wings, ground poultry, and stuffing)	165 °F (73.9 °C)
Eggs	160 °F (71.1 °C)
Fish & shellfish	145 °F (62.8 °C)
Leftovers	165 °F (73.9 °C)
Casseroles	165 °F (73.9 °C)

Tips and Tricks for Success

The most important thing to remember as you pursue this new lifestyle is to go slow. You must be patient with yourself at every turn: Train yourself to slow down and read every label when shopping. Take the time to explore different brands and flavors and find the ones you like. You're not giving up the foods you love, just changing them.

Get familiar with the manager of your local grocery store—they can often order more low-sodium goods on request. Your butcher can supply you with the freshest proteins that have not been salted or over processed.

Stay away from sugary drinks, and jazz up your water by infusing. Try adding fresh fruit, vegetables, and herbs to water, such as apple and cinnamon sticks, orange and raspberries, mixed berries, cucumber and mint, carrots and apples, fennel and pear, and cilantro and citrus. Experiment! Infusing naturally flavors water without adding salt or sugar.

Make lists before you go shopping, plan out your meals for the week if possible, and determine what you will need ahead of time. Planning is a huge step in preventing temptation at the grocery store. You will venture down new aisles, explore new products, read labels, and examine contents. These first few shopping trips may take a bit longer than usual, but "usual" is killing you.

Do your prep work when you get home from the grocery store. Wash your vegetables and cut them into grab-and-go size sticks for quick snacks. If you know your menu over the next few days, wash any veggies you need, cut them up as called for in the recipes, and keep them separate in bags. When the time comes, it'll be so easy to put that healthy meal together.

If you know that you will be regularly using certain portions, pre-portion in plastic bags and repack in the original box. That way, when it's time to cook, you just grab and go.

Easy is the name of the game here. Whatever is easiest for you, whatever saves you time and makes things more flavorful for you, will help you stay with this new lifestyle and see it less as a "diet," but a way of life. Let's get real. Let's get healthy together.

Oven-Roasted Vegetables with Rosemary p.80

3

THE MEAL PLANS

The meal plans presented on the following pages will help you to ease into your new way of eating. For each day, a suggested breakfast, lunch, and dinner is presented using the recipes in this book. The goal is to limit your total sodium intake for the day to approximately 1,500 mg. You can think in terms of 500 mg of sodium per meal or less, taking into account any additional foods you eat, such as snacks. The menus are to be used as a guide, so feel free to swap out recipes for the ones that appeal to you the most.

Be patient. Changing food habits is a skill that takes time and practice. It takes taste buds three weeks or more to lose their taste for sodium.

Low-Sodium Meal Plan for Hypertension / High Blood Pressure

Reducing sodium in the diet can prevent high blood pressure for those at risk for the disease and can help control blood pressure. Limiting sodium is part of a heart-healthy eating plan that can help prevent heart disease and stroke. If you limit your sodium intake to 1,500 mg per day, you can lower your blood pressure.

Week 1

Sunday

Breakfast: Slow-Cooker French Toast (p. 54)

Lunch: Mixed Baby Greens with Peaches, Fennel, and Walnuts (p. 96)

Dinner: Roasted Salmon with Spinach-Quinoa Salad (p. 148)

Snacks: Greek yogurt and berries

Monday

Breakfast: Leftover Slow-Cooker French Toast (p. 54)

Lunch: Greek Omelet (p. 126)

Dinner: Slow-Cooker Turkey Chili (p. 94)

Snacks: Kale Chips (p. 76) and Traditional Hummus (p. 78)

Tuesday

Breakfast: Overnight Spiced Oatmeal with Cranberries (p. 59)

Lunch: Leftover Slow-Cooker Turkey Chili (p. 94)

Dinner: Leftover Roasted Salmon with Spinach-Quinoa Salad (p. 148)

Snacks: Hard-boiled egg and piece of fruit

Wednesday

Breakfast: Chorizo Sweet Potato Hash (p. 66)

Lunch: Leftover Greek Omelet (p. 126)

Dinner: Eggplant "Parmesan" Marinara (p. 132)

Snacks: Fresh fruit and unsalted almonds

Thursday

Breakfast: Avocado Toast with Basil Pesto (p. 64)

Lunch: Leftover Eggplant "Parmesan" Marinara (p. 132)

Dinner: Cauliflower Fried Rice (p. 116)

Snacks: Greek yogurt and berries

Friday

Breakfast: Creamy Blueberry-Banana Smoothie (p. 58)

Lunch: Leftover Cauliflower Fried Rice (p. 116)

Dinner: Pork Medallions with Herbes de Provence (p. 180)

Snacks: Edamame and baby carrots

Saturday

Breakfast: Overnight Oatmeal with Banana and Chocolate (p. 60)

Lunch: Sweet Potato Egg Cups (p. 124)

Dinner: Slow-Cooker Chickpea Vegetable Stew (p. 109)

Snacks: Kale Chips (p. 76) and Traditional Hummus (p. 78)

Week 2

Sunday

Breakfast: Slow-Cooker Quinoa and Oats (p. 56)

Lunch: Sweet Potato Egg Cups (p. 124)

Dinner: Turkey and Wild Rice (p. 182)

Snacks: Simple Roasted Chickpeas (p. 77)

Monday

Breakfast: Leftover Slow-Cooker Quinoa and Oats (p. 56)

Lunch: Leftover Turkey and Wild Rice (p. 182)

Dinner: Leftover Slow-Cooker Chickpea Vegetable Stew (p. 109)

Snacks: Kale Chips (p. 76)

Tuesday

Breakfast: Overnight Spiced Oatmeal with Cranberries (p. 59)

Lunch: Leftover Sweet Potato Egg Cups (p. 124)

Dinner: Shrimp and Black Bean Salad (p. 152)

Snacks: Edamame

Wednesday

Breakfast: Avocado Toast with Basil Pesto (p. 64)

Lunch: Leftover Shrimp and Black Bean Salad (p. 152)

Dinner: Slow-Cooker Red Beans and Rice (p. 112)

Snacks: Simple Roasted Chickpeas (p. 77)

Thursday

Breakfast: Creamy Blueberry-Banana Smoothie (p. 58)

Lunch: Leftover Slow-Cooker Red Beans and Rice (p. 112)

Dinner: Fish Tacos with Mango Salsa (p. 150)

Snacks: Greek yogurt and berries

Friday

Breakfast: Honey-Lime Quinoa Fruit Salad (p. 61)

Lunch: Leftover Fish Tacos with Mango Salsa (p. 150)

Dinner: Slow-Cooker Tortilla Chicken Soup (p. 93)

Snacks: Hard-boiled egg and vegetable sticks

Saturday

Breakfast: Chorizo Sweet Potato Hash (p. 66)

Lunch: Simple Southwest Tofu Scramble (p. 128)

Dinner: Slow-Cooker Bison Tacos (p. 166)

Snacks: Fresh fruit and unsalted nuts

Week 3

Sunday

Breakfast: Slow-Cooker Vegetable Frittata (p. 57)

Lunch: Cod with Tomato-Thyme Salsa (p. 142)

Dinner: Broccoli, Peas, and Whole Grain Rigatoni (p. 113)

Snacks: Traditional Hummus (p. 78) and vegetable sticks

Monday

Breakfast: Leftover Slow-Cooker Vegetable Frittata (p. 57)

Lunch: Leftover Broccoli, Peas, and Whole Grain Rigatoni (p. 113)

Dinner: Leftover Slow-Cooker Bison Tacos (p. 166)

Snacks: Greek yogurt and berries

Tuesday

Breakfast: Creamy Blueberry-Banana Smoothie (p. 58)

Lunch: Lemon Pepper Salmon in Foil (p. 155)

Dinner: Slow-Cooker Shredded Root Beer Beef (p. 167)

Snacks: Traditional Hummus (p. 78) and vegetable sticks

Wednesday

Breakfast: Overnight Spiced Oatmeal with Cranberries (p. 59)

Lunch: Leftover Slow-Cooker Shredded Root Beer Beef (p. 167)

Dinner: Cabbage-Stuffed Flounder (p. 144)

Snacks: Hard-boiled egg and vegetable sticks

Thursday

Breakfast: Chorizo Sweet Potato Hash (p. 66)

Lunch: Leftover Cabbage-Stuffed Flounder (p. 144)

Dinner: Polenta with Fresh Vegetables (p. 118)

Snacks: Unsalted nuts and fresh fruit

Friday

Breakfast: Overnight Oatmeal with Banana and Chocolate (p. 60)

Lunch: Leftover Polenta with Fresh Vegetables (p. 118)

Dinner: Southwestern Veggie Bowl (p. 114)

Snacks: Chocolate Chia Seed Pudding (p. 195)

Saturday

Breakfast: Avocado Toast with Basil Pesto (p. 64)

Lunch: English Cucumber Salad (p. 97)

Dinner: Slow-Cooker Curry Chicken (p. 169)

Snacks: Unsalted nuts and fresh fruit

Week 4

Sunday

Breakfast: Orange-Almond Muffins (p. 62)

Lunch: Creole-Style Black-Eyed Peas with Spinach (p. 120)

Dinner: New York Strip Steak with Mushroom Sauce (p. 175)

Snacks: Lemon Thins (p. 190)

Monday

Breakfast: Avocado Toast with Basil Pesto (p. 64)

Lunch: Greek Omelet (p. 126)

Dinner: Leftover Slow-Cooker Curry Chicken (p. 169)

Snacks: Slow-Cooker Spiced Nuts (p. 75)

Tuesday

Breakfast: Orange-Almond Muffins (p. 62)

Lunch: Leftover Creole-Style Black-Eyed Peas with Spinach (p. 120)

Dinner: Greek Fish in a Packet (p.156)

Snacks: Fresh fruit and Greek yogurt

Wednesday

Breakfast: Overnight Oatmeal with Banana and Chocolate (p. 60)

Lunch: Leftover Greek Fish in a Packet (p. 156)

Dinner: Eggplant "Parmesan" Marinara (p. 132)

Snacks: Slow-Cooker Spiced Nuts (p. 75)

Thursday

Breakfast: Orange-Almond Muffins (p. 62)

Lunch: Leftover Eggplant "Parmesan" Marinara (p. 132)

Dinner: Lemon Quinoa and Peas (p. 133)

Snacks: Kale Chips (p. 76) and hard-boiled egg

Friday

Breakfast: Creamy Blueberry-Banana Smoothie (p. 58)

Lunch: Leftover Lemon Quinoa and Peas (p. 133)

Dinner: Chili and Red Pepper–Crusted Scallops (p. 154)

Snacks: Slow-Cooker Spiced Nuts (p. 75)

Saturday

Breakfast: Sweet Potato Egg Cups (p. 124)

Lunch: Mixed Baby Greens with Peaches, Fennel, and Walnuts (p. 96)

Dinner: Slow-Cooker Pork Chops and Potatoes (p. 174)

Snacks: Banana Ice Cream (p. 192)

Low-Sodium Meal Plan for Congestive Heart Failure

If you have congestive heart failure, check food labels, and limit salt and sodium to approximately 1,500 mg per day. Focus on fresh fruits and vegetables, choose meats low in saturated fat, and if your heart failure is caused by alcohol, its especially important that you don't drink alcoholic beverages. Aim for 500 mg of sodium per meal, and choose fresh fruits, vegetables, and unsalted nuts for snacks.

Week 1

Sunday

Breakfast: Slow-Cooker Quinoa and Oats (p. 56)

Lunch: Sweet Potato Egg Cups (p. 124)

Dinner: Pan Seared Salmon with Balsamic-Rosemary Roasted Vegetables (p. 146)

Snacks: Fresh fruit and unsalted nuts

Monday

Breakfast: Leftover Slow-Cooker Quinoa and Oats (p. 56)

Lunch: Leftover Pan Seared Salmon with Balsamic-Rosemary Roasted Vegetables (p. 146)

Dinner: Slow-Cooker Red Beans and Rice (p. 112)

Snacks: Traditional Hummus (p. 78) and vegetable sticks

Tuesday

Breakfast: Overnight Spiced Oatmeal with Cranberries (p. 59)

Lunch: Leftover Slow-Cooker Red Beans and Rice (p. 112)

Dinner: Cabbage-Stuffed Flounder (p. 144)

Snacks: Cinnamon Oranges (p. 189)

Wednesday

Breakfast: Creamy Blueberry-Banana Smoothie (p. 58)

Lunch: Leftover Cabbage-Stuffed Flounder (p. 144)

Dinner: Black Bean Croquettes with Fresh Salsa (p. 122)

Snacks: Hard-boiled egg and vegetable sticks

Thursday

Breakfast: Honey-Lime Quinoa Fruit Salad (p. 61)

Lunch: Leftover Black Bean Croquettes with Fresh Salsa (p. 122)

Dinner: Chili and Red Pepper–Crusted Scallops (p. 154)

Snacks: Cinnamon Oranges (p. 189)

Friday

Breakfast: Avocado Toast with Basil Pesto (p. 64)

Lunch: Leftover Chili and Red Pepper–Crusted Scallops (p. 154)

Dinner: Slow-Cooker Lemon-Garlic Chicken (p. 172)

Snacks: Edamame

Saturday

Breakfast: Overnight Oatmeal with Banana and Chocolate (p. 60)

Lunch: Mixed Baby Greens with Peaches, Fennel, and Walnuts (p. 96)

Dinner: Slow-Cooker Apple Pork Loin (p. 164)

Snacks: Fresh fruit and Greek yogurt

Week 2

Sunday

Breakfast: Orange-Almond Muffins (p. 62)

Lunch: Leftover Slow-Cooker Lemon-Garlic Chicken (p. 172)

Dinner: Greek Fish in a Packet (p. 156)

Snacks: Fresh fruit and unsalted nuts

Monday

Breakfast: Overnight Oatmeal with Banana and Chocolate (p. 60)

Lunch: Leftover Slow-Cooker Apple Pork Loin (p. 164)

Dinner: Slow-Cooker Sweet and Sour Chicken (p. 168)

Snacks: Banana Ice Cream (p. 192)

Tuesday

Breakfast: Orange-Almond Muffins (p. 62)

Lunch: Leftover Slow-Cooker Sweet and Sour Chicken (p. 168)

Dinner: Shrimp and Black Bean Salad (p. 152)

Snacks: Hard-boiled egg and vegetable sticks

Wednesday

Breakfast: Overnight Spiced Oatmeal with Cranberries (p. 59)

Lunch: Leftover Shrimp and Black Bean Salad (p. 152)

Dinner: Eggplant "Parmesan" Marinara (p. 132)

Snacks: Banana Ice Cream (p. 192)

Thursday

Breakfast: Orange-Almond Muffins (p. 62)

Lunch: Leftover Eggplant "Parmesan" Marinara (p. 132)

Dinner: Pork Medallions with Herbes de Provence (p. 180)

Snacks: Edamame

Friday

Breakfast: Creamy Blueberry-Banana Smoothie (p. 58)

Lunch: Leftover Pork Medallions with Herbes de Provence (p. 180)

Dinner: Slow-Cooker Quinoa–Black Bean Stuffed Peppers (p. 102)

Snacks: Greek yogurt and berries

Saturday

Breakfast: Chorizo Sweet Potato Hash (p. 66)

Lunch: Leftover Slow-Cooker Quinoa–Black Bean Stuffed Peppers (p. 102)

Dinner: Lemon Pepper Salmon in Foil (p. 155)

Snacks: Kale Chips (p. 76)

Week 3

Sunday

Breakfast: Slow-Cooker French Toast (p. 54)

Lunch: Simple Southwest Tofu Scramble (p. 128)

Dinner: Roasted Salmon with Spinach-Quinoa Salad (p. 148)

Snacks: Cinnamon Oranges (p. 189)

Monday

Breakfast: Leftover Slow-Cooker French Toast (p. 54)

Lunch: Roasted Salmon with Spinach-Quinoa Salad (p. 148)

Dinner: Cauliflower Fried Rice (p. 116)

Snacks: Traditional Hummus (p. 78) and Kale Chips (p. 76)

Tuesday

Breakfast: Honey-Lime Quinoa Fruit Salad (p. 61)

Lunch: Leftover Cauliflower Fried Rice (p. 116)

Dinner: Slow-Cooker Hawaiian Chicken (p. 160)

Snacks: Hard-boiled egg and vegetable sticks

Wednesday

Breakfast: Overnight Spiced Oatmeal with Cranberries (p. 59)

Lunch: Leftover Slow-Cooker Hawaiian Chicken (p. 160)

Dinner: Chili and Red Pepper–Crusted Scallops (p. 154)

Snacks: Fresh fruit and Greek yogurt

Thursday

Breakfast: Creamy Blueberry-Banana Smoothie (p. 58)

Lunch: Leftover Chili and Red Pepper–Crusted Scallops (p. 154)

Dinner: Slow-Cooker Pork Chops and Potatoes (p. 174)

Snacks: Unsalted nuts and vegetable sticks

Friday

Breakfast: Avocado Toast with Basil Pesto (p. 64)

Lunch: Leftover Slow-Cooker Pork Chops and Potatoes (p. 174)

Dinner: Fish Tacos with Mango Salsa (p. 150)

Snacks: Fresh fruit and Greek yogurt

Saturday

Breakfast: Slow-Cooker Quinoa and Oats (p. 56)

Lunch: Leftover Fish Tacos with Mango Salsa (p. 150)

Dinner: Southwestern Veggie Bowl (p. 114)

Snacks: Banana Ice Cream (p. 192)

Week 4

Sunday

Breakfast: Slow-Cooker Vegetable Frittata (p. 57)

Lunch: English Cucumber Salad (p. 97)

Dinner: Slow-Cooker Lemon-Garlic Chicken (p. 172)

Snacks: Lemon Thins (p. 190)

Monday

Breakfast: Leftover Slow-Cooker Vegetable Frittata (p. 57)

Lunch: Leftover Slow-Cooker Lemon-Garlic Chicken (p. 172)

Dinner: Cabbage-Stuffed Flounder (p. 144)

Snacks: Lemon Thins (p. 190)

Tuesday

Breakfast: Avocado Toast with Basil Pesto (p. 64)

Lunch: Leftover Cabbage-Stuffed Flounder (p. 144)

Dinner: Lemon Quinoa and Peas (p. 133)

Snacks: Banana Ice Cream (p. 192)

Wednesday

Breakfast: Overnight Spiced Oatmeal with Cranberries (p. 59)

Lunch: Leftover Lemon Quinoa and Peas (p. 133)

Dinner: Slow-Cooker Turkey Chili (p. 94)

Snacks: Edamame

Thursday

Breakfast: Chorizo Sweet Potato Hash (p. 66)

Lunch: Leftover Slow-Cooker Turkey Chili (p. 94)

Dinner: Broccoli, Peas, and Whole Grain Rigatoni (p. 113)

Snacks: Hard-boiled egg and vegetable sticks

Friday

Breakfast: Creamy Blueberry-Banana Smoothie (p. 58)

Lunch: Leftover Broccoli, Peas, and Whole Grain Rigatoni (p. 113)

Dinner: Slow-Cooker Red Beans and Rice (p. 112)

Snacks: Baked Apples with Cherries and Walnuts (p. 186)

Saturday

Breakfast: Overnight Oatmeal with Banana and Chocolate (p. 60)

Lunch: Leftover Slow-Cooker Red Beans and Rice (p. 112)

Dinner: Pork Medallions with Herbes de Provence (p. 180)

Snacks: Greek yogurt and fresh fruit

About the Recipes

Each of the recipes in this book has a label highlighting its nutritional attributes. The labels can help you to quickly and easily identify recipes that meet your individual preferences and dietary needs. Each recipe will have one or more of the following labels:

Meatless: The recipe does not contain any meat and is a vegetarian dish.

Dairy-Free: The recipe does not contain any dairy ingredients including milk, butter, or cheese.

Gluten-Free: The recipe does not contain any gluten-containing ingredients or ingredient substitutions can be made to make it gluten-free.

Low-Fat: This label means the recipe will use very little oil or fat and usually contains 3 grams of fat or less per serving.

One-Pot: This label means you will only need one pot, pan, bowl, blender, etc. to complete the dish.

Additionally, each recipe is marked as "low," "lower," or "lowest" sodium. This is to help you manage your sodium intake without a lot of fuss. If you're interested in a "low" sodium recipe but had a higher-sodium snack earlier in the day, consider a "lower" or "lowest" sodium recipe instead. The breakdown is as follows:

PART
2

THE RECIPES

Indian Mango Chutney p.46

4

BROTHS, SAUCES, SPICE MIXES, AND DRESSINGS

Slow-Cooker Vegetable Broth

Makes 8 cups / Prep time: 10 minutes / Cook time: 8 hours, plus 10 minutes cooling time

Slow-cooker vegetable broth tastes amazing, costs pennies to make, and is free of added preservatives and stabilizers. Because you control the ingredients, you can ensure a low-sodium content, use fresh ingredients, and keep the flavor rich. Use this broth as a base for soups or to elevate grain and rice dishes.

2 carrots, chopped
2 celery stalks, chopped
2 onions, chopped
1 large tomato, chopped
3 garlic cloves, halved
½ cup chopped mixed mushrooms

2 bay leaves
¼ teaspoon freshly ground
   black pepper
⅓ cup chopped fresh parsley
7 cups water

1. In a slow cooker, add all the ingredients and stir to combine. Cover and cook on low for 8 hours, until the broth is golden and the vegetables are very tender.

2. Remove the lid from the slow cooker and let the broth cool for 10 to 15 minutes.

3. Use a wooden spoon to gently press on the veggies in the slow cooker to release a little more flavor.

4. Strain the broth by it pouring into a colander set on top of a large bowl, pressing the vegetables to extract liquid. Discard the cooked vegetables.

5. Refrigerate uncovered until cool, then cover.

Tip: You can also use a mix of frozen vegetables for the broth or a combination of fresh scraps and frozen vegetables. Potato peels can also be added to the mix for additional flavor.

Storage: The broth will keep in the refrigerator in an airtight container for up to 5 days. For longer storage, freeze in heavy-duty freezer bags for up to 1 month.

PER SERVING (1 cup) Calories: 28; Total Fat 0g; Saturated Fat: 0g; Cholesterol: 0mg; Sodium: 0mg; Potassium: 220mg; Total Carbohydrate: 6g; Fiber: 2g; Protein: 1g

Slow-Cooker Fresh Tomato Pasta Sauce

Makes 4 cups / Prep time: 15 minutes
Cook time: 6 to 10 hours, plus 15 minute cooling time

MEATLESS
DAIRY-FREE
GLUTEN-FREE
LOW-FAT
ONE-POT

A low-sodium diet doesn't mean giving up your favorite sauces. This very low-sodium pasta sauce uses fresh tomatoes, no canned ingredients, and gets it bold flavors from fresh herbs and spices. Customize it by adding your favorite vegetables or meat, if desired, and use it on pasta, rice, or potatoes.

5 pounds tomatoes (such as Roma), quartered

4 garlic cloves, crushed

1 medium onion, roughly chopped

1 medium carrot, roughly chopped

1 dried bay leaf

4 tablespoons chopped fresh basil

2 tablespoons chopped fresh oregano

1 tablespoon chopped fresh parsley

1 teaspoon chopped fresh thyme

½ teaspoon chopped fresh rosemary

1 pinch red pepper flakes

2 tablespoons extra-virgin olive oil

Freshly ground black pepper

1 teaspoon honey (optional)

1. In a slow cooker, add the tomatoes, garlic, onion, carrot, bay leaf, basil, oregano, parsley, thyme, rosemary, and red pepper flakes. Drizzle the olive oil over the tomatoes and herbs. Cover and cook on low for 2 to 4 hours, stirring occasionally.

2. After the sauce has simmered and the tomatoes have released their juices, turn off the slow cooker and allow the sauce to cool.

3. Run the cooled tomato sauce through a food strainer to remove the skins, seeds, and to smooth out the sauce.

4. Return the strained tomato sauce to the slow cooker, set the slow cooker on low, and vent the lid so excess moisture evaporates. Cook until desired thickness is reached, 4 to 6 hours or longer, stirring occasionally.

5. Once the tomato sauce is thick, season lightly with the black pepper. If the flavor is too sharp and acidic, add a teaspoon of honey (if using).

Tip: If you are including additional ingredients such as mushrooms, green peppers, sausage, or meatballs, precook these and add them to the slow cooker after step 5 and cook on low for an additional 1 to 2 hours.

Storage: The tomato sauce can be stored in the refrigerator in an airtight covered container for 3 to 4 days. To further extend the shelf life, freeze in covered airtight containers or heavy-duty freezer bags and use within one year.

PER SERVING (½ cup) Calories: 102; Total Fat 4g; Saturated Fat: 1g; Cholesterol: 0mg; Sodium: 0mg; Potassium: 698mg; Total Carbohydrate: 16g; Fiber: 4g; Protein: 3g

Slow-Cooker Salsa

SODIUM

LOWEST

MEATLESS
DAIRY-FREE
GLUTEN-FREE
LOW-FAT
ONE-POT

Makes 4 cups / Prep time: 15 minutes
Cook time: 2 hours 30 minutes on high, plus 1 hour cooling time

This refreshing homemade salsa is versatile enough to top sandwiches, soups, savory recipes, grains, and vegetables, in addition to traditional uses on burritos, tacos, chips, and more. Made with fresh ingredients, Roma tomatoes, and shallots to add depth to the bright flavors in this easy and uncomplicated recipe.

1 medium white onion, chopped
4 pounds Roma tomatoes, quartered
6 garlic cloves, minced
1 large shallot, quartered

2 fresh habanero, jalapeño, or serrano peppers (more if you like your salsa hot), seeds removed
½ cup fresh cilantro leaves
1 tablespoon freshly squeezed lime juice

1. In a slow cooker, spread the onion in the bottom of the crock.
2. Add the tomatoes, garlic, shallot, and peppers. Cover and cook on high for 2½ hours, stirring occasionally so the shallot does not stick to the sides.
3. When the time is up, turn off the slow cooker, take off the lid, and let cool for about 1 hour.
4. When cooled, transfer to a blender. Add the cilantro and lime juice, and pulse to the desired consistency. Serve immediately.

Variation Tip: You can easily make this into a fruit or bean salsa by adding ½ cup of your favorite fresh fruit or ½ cup drained and rinsed beans after blending.

Storage: Store in an airtight, covered container in the refrigerator for 1 week. You can also freeze in heavy-duty freezer bags or freezer safe containers for up to 3 months.

PER SERVING (2 tablespoons) Calories: 15; Total Fat 0g; Saturated Fat: 0g; Cholesterol: 0mg; Sodium: 5mg; Potassium: 136mg; Total Carbohydrate: 3g; Fiber: 1g; Protein: 1g

Slow-Cooker Cranberry Sauce

Makes 1¼ cups / Prep time: 5 minutes / Cook time: 3 hours

SODIUM

LOWEST

MEATLESS
DAIRY-FREE
GLUTEN-FREE
LOW-FAT
ONE-POT

Cranberries are one of the richest sources of phytonutrients that offer antioxidant, anti-inflammatory, and cardiovascular health benefits, and are readily available year round in most supermarkets. With no added sugars or salt, enjoy this nutritious sauce on Thanksgiving and all year long in smoothies, stirred into muffin batters or oatmeal, and as a sauce for pan-fried steak or roasted chicken breasts.

1 (12-ounce) bag fresh cranberries

½ cup freshly squeezed
   orange juice

½ cup water

¼ cup honey

1 cinnamon stick

Pinch ground cinnamon

Pinch ground ginger

1. In a slow cooker, add all the ingredients and toss to combine.

2. Cook on low for 3 to 4 hours, and stir with a wooden spoon or spatula near the end of cooking to break up the cranberries. The sauce will thicken as it cools.

Storage: You can store homemade cranberry sauce in the refrigerator in a covered container for 10 to 14 days. You can also freeze the sauce for 2 months.

PER SERVING (2 tablespoons) Calories: 38; Total Fat 0g; Saturated Fat: 0g; Cholesterol: 0mg; Sodium: 1mg; Potassium: 40mg; Total Carbohydrate: 10g; Fiber: 1g; Protein: 0g

Indian Mango Chutney

Makes 2 cups / Prep time: 5 minutes / Cook time: 8 minutes

Not only is mango delicious, it has numerous health benefits, boasting high amounts of antioxidant vitamins A and E, and is rich in cholesterol-lowering fiber. Traditional Indian recipes use jaggery, a naturally processed sugar from the sap of sugar cane or palm trees. You can find jaggery in Indian groceries or substitute with white sugar.

1 tablespoon peanut oil
½ teaspoon panch phoran, or
    equal amount mix of ground
    cumin, ground fennel, mustard,
    fenugreek
1 tablespoon grated fresh ginger

2 medium semi-ripe mangoes,
    peeled, seeded, and
    finely chopped
¼ teaspoon red chili powder
⅛ teaspoon garam masala
½ teaspoon ground cloves
2 tablespoons jaggery or
    white sugar

1. In a medium skillet, heat the oil over medium-high heat. Add the panch phoran (or equivalent spice mix) and fry gently while stirring, until fragrant, 1 to 2 minutes.

2. Add the ginger and continue cooking for another 1 minute.

3. Add the mango, the red chili powder, garam masala, and the cloves. Stir and simmer for 1 to 2 minutes.

4. Add the jaggery (or sugar) and stir and cook for an additional 2 to 3 minutes. Don't overcook, as the mixture will become thick.

5. Transfer the mango chutney to a serving bowl and serve warm or at room temperature as a dip or spread.

Storage: Store the mango chutney in an airtight container in the refrigerator where it will keep for 2 to 3 days.

PER SERVING (2 tablespoons) Calories: 27; Total Fat 1g; Saturated Fat: 0g; Cholesterol: 0mg; Sodium: 1mg; Potassium: 35mg; Total Carbohydrate: 5g; Fiber: 0g; Protein: 0g

Texas-Style BBQ Dry Rub

Makes 1 ¼ cup / Prep time: 5 minutes

SODIUM

LOWEST

MEATLESS
DAIRY-FREE
GLUTEN-FREE
LOW-FAT
ONE-POT

Texas-style leans more towards the smoky and sweet flavors of barbeque. A rub is typically applied to your protein before cooking and pairs nicely with sweeter barbeque sauce or ketchup.

½ cup raw turbinado sugar

¼ cup Hungarian paprika

2 tablespoons granulated garlic

2 tablespoons granulated onion

2 tablespoons freshly ground black pepper

1 tablespoon salt-free chili powder

1 tablespoon cayenne pepper

1. In a large Mason jar, add all the ingredients.

2. Seal the jar and shake until well mixed.

PER SERVING (1 tablespoon) Calories: 39; Total Fat 0g; Saturated Fat: 0g; Cholesterol: 0mg; Sodium: 5mg; Potassium: 53mg; Total Carbohydrate: 9g; Fiber: 1g; Protein: 0g

Tequila-Lime Marinade

Makes 1 cup / Prep time: 5 minutes

In Florida it's a tradition to hoist a margarita and toast a sunset. When I was a bachelor and first learning to cook, the ingredients in a margarita made a perfect marinade for chicken and fish. Most of the alcohol cooks off, imparting a nice flavor to the citrus juice and olive oil to season the fish.

½ cup extra-virgin olive oil
¼ cup freshly squeezed lime juice
¼ cup tequila

¼ cup freshly squeezed
orange juice
4 garlic cloves, minced

In a nonreactive glass bowl, add all the ingredients and stir to combine.

Tip: Completely immerse your proteins in marinade for at least 30 minutes in the refrigerator.

PER SERVING (2 tablespoons) Calories: 141; Total Fat 13g; Saturated Fat: 2g; Cholesterol: 0mg; Sodium: 0mg; Potassium: 21mg; Total Carbohydrate: 1g; Fiber: 0g; Protein: 0g

Taco Seasoning

Makes 1 cup / Prep time: 10 minutes

I've used this seasoning on so much more than tacos; I've used it on steaks, burgers, chicken, and fish. Once you make your own seasoning you'll never go back to buying store packets again. Our kids love to measure the spices and shake the jar to mix it up.

10 tablespoons chili powder

6 teaspoons freshly ground black pepper

6 teaspoons cumin

3 teaspoons ground coriander

3 teaspoons pimentón (Spanish paprika)

1½ teaspoons garlic powder

1½ teaspoons onion powder

1½ teaspoons dried oregano

¾ teaspoon ground red pepper (optional)

1. In a large mason jar, add all the ingredients.
2. Seal the jar and shake until well mixed.

PER SERVING (1 tablespoon) Calories: 21; Total Fat 1g; Saturated Fat: 0g; Cholesterol: 0mg; Sodium: 48mg; Potassium: 120mg; Total Carbohydrate: 4g; Fiber: 2g; Protein: 1g

SODIUM

LOWEST

MEATLESS
DAIRY-FREE
GLUTEN-FREE
LOW-FAT
ONE-POT

Low-Sodium Mayonnaise

Makes 2 cups / Prep Time: 10 minutes

Store-bought mayonnaise is typically loaded with sodium. If you just can't live without mayo, then this recipe will satisfy your craving, without the sodium overload.

2 large eggs

2 to 3 tablespoons white wine vinegar, or desired vinegar

2 teaspoons ground mustard

½ teaspoon freshly ground black pepper

½ teaspoon garlic powder

½ teaspoon paprika

¼ teaspoon cayenne pepper

1 to 2 cups extra-virgin olive oil

1. In a blender, break the eggs and add the vinegar, mustard, black pepper, garlic powder, paprika, and cayenne.

2. Run the blender at its slowest speed until the ingredients are well mixed.

3. Keeping the blender running, slowly add the oil in a steady stream, increasing the speed of the blender as the mayonnaise thickens so it is emulsified.

4. Store the mayonnaise in a sealed container in the refrigerator for two weeks.

Tip: You can also substitute low-cholesterol Egg Beaters (2 eggs' worth).

PER SERVING (2 tablespoons) Calories: 190; Total Fat 21g; Saturated Fat: 3g; Cholesterol: 23mg; Sodium: 24mg; Potassium: 14mg; Total Carbohydrate: 0g; Fiber: 0g; Protein: 1g

Low-Sodium French Dressing

Makes 2 cups / Prep Time: 10 minutes

This is my mom's favorite salad dressing. It also makes a great stand-alone dip for vegetables.

¾ cup low-sodium tomato juice

½ cup apple cider vinegar

Juice of 1 lemon

1 garlic clove, minced

¼ onion, chopped

2 teaspoons mustard powder

½ teaspoon cumin

½ teaspoon paprika

4 packets artificial sweetener of choice

½ cup extra-virgin olive oil

1. In a blender, add the tomato juice, vinegar, lemon juice, garlic, and onion, and blend until puréed.

2. Add the mustard powder, cumin, paprika, and sweetener, and blend at low speed.

3. Increase the speed and slowly add the oil, blending to emulsify.

4. Store in a sealed container in the refrigerator for up to two weeks.

PER SERVING (2 tablespoons) Calories: 63; Total Fat 7g; Saturated Fat: 1g; Cholesterol: 0mg; Sodium: 7mg; Potassium: 50mg; Total Carbohydrate: 1g; Fiber: 0g; Protein: 0g

Overnight Spiced Oatmeal with Cranberries p.59

5

BREAKFASTS

Slow-Cooker French Toast

Serves 6 / Prep time: 15 minutes
Cook time: 2 to 2 hours and 30 minutes on high, 7 hours on low

A slow cooker does all the work for you in this delicious and nutritious recipe for French toast. Healthier and much easier to prepare than traditional French toast, assemble this recipe at night before you go to bed and enjoy waking up to a sweet and moist breakfast without all the fuss.

FOR THE FILLING

2 tablespoons honey

½ cup low-fat ricotta cheese

⅓ cup sliced almonds

½ teaspoon cinnamon

3 cups finely diced apples pieces

FOR THE FRENCH TOAST

Cooking spray

2 eggs

2 egg whites

1½ cups nonfat milk (or almond
  or soy milk)

1 tablespoon honey

1 teaspoon vanilla extract

½ teaspoon cinnamon

12 slices light whole-grain bread,
  lightly toasted

TO MAKE THE FILLING

To make the filling, in a large bowl mix together the honey, ricotta cheese, almonds, and cinnamon until uniform. Add the apples and stir to coat.

TO MAKE THE FRENCH TOAST

1. Spray the inside of a slow cooker with nonstick cooking spray.

2. In a medium bowl, whisk together the eggs, egg whites, milk, honey, vanilla, and cinnamon.

3. Tear the toasted bread into 1-inch squares. Place ⅓ of the bread in the bottom of the slow cooker. Top with ⅓ of the filling mixture. Repeat twice with the remaining bread and apple mixture.

4. Pour the egg mixture over the contents of the slow cooker. Cook on high for 2 to 2½ hours, or on low for 7 hours, until set.

Storage: You can keep French toast in the refrigerator for 3 to 5 days, or store in the freezer for several weeks. Reheat in a skillet on the stove top over medium heat to recrisp the exterior.

PER SERVING Calories: 228; Total Fat 5g; Saturated Fat: 2g; Cholesterol: 63mg; Sodium: 238mg; Potassium: 261mg; Total Carbohydrate: 36g; Fiber: 6g; Protein: 12g

Slow-Cooker Quinoa and Oats

Serves 6 / Prep time: 5 minutes / Cook time: 2 hours on high, 6 to 7 hours on low

Quinoa is a very versatile grain, high in fiber, protein, and antioxidants, and in this recipe it is mixed with equally nutritious steel-cut oats for an overnight breakfast sensation, without added sugars or salt. Perfectly fluffy and delicious, with barely any prep time, enjoy waking up to this healthy breakfast.

1 cup gluten-free steel-cut oats

½ cup quinoa, rinsed

4½ cups unsweetened vanilla almond milk (or water), plus more for serving

4 Medjool dates, chopped

1 apple peeled and diced

2 teaspoons cinnamon

¼ teaspoon nutmeg

1 teaspoon vanilla extract

¼ cup crushed walnuts (optional)

1. Spray the inside of a slow cooker with nonstick spray.

2. Combine the steel-cut oats, quinoa, almond milk, dates, apple, cinnamon, nutmeg, and vanilla in the slow cooker.

3. Cook on high for 2 hours, or on low for 6 to 7 hours.

4. Stir well before serving. Top each serving with walnuts (if using) and a splash of almond milk.

Tip: Medjool dates are used to add sweetness, vitamins, minerals, and fiber. You could replace the dates with brown sugar, honey, or maple syrup, if desired.

Storage: Leftover quinoa and oats can be stored in a covered container in the refrigerator for 3 to 5 days. You can also freeze leftovers for several months by portioning into plastic freezer bags.

PER SERVING Calories: 230; Total Fat 5g; Saturated Fat: 0g; Cholesterol: 0mg; Sodium: 119mg; Potassium: 212mg; Total Carbohydrate: 44g; Fiber: 6g; Protein: 7g

Slow-Cooker Vegetable Frittata

Serves 6 / Prep time: 10 minutes / Cook time: 1 to 1½ hours on low

This nutrient-rich frittata is filled with heart-healthy vegetables and high protein eggs. The slow cooking time infuses the eggs with the other ingredients' flavors, so go ahead and add your favorites.

1 tablespoon extra-virgin olive oil

½ cup sliced green onion

1 medium red bell pepper, chopped

2 garlic cloves, minced

1 cup shredded part skim mozzarella cheese, divided

3 eggs

3 egg whites

2 tablespoons milk (nonfat, almond, or soy)

1 packed cup chopped baby kale, stems removed

1 Roma tomato, diced

¼ teaspoon freshly ground black pepper

¼ cup chopped fresh parsley, for garnish

1. In a small skillet, heat the oil over medium heat.

2. Sauté the onion, bell pepper, and garlic until tender and fragrant, about 5 minutes.

3. Lightly spray the inside of a slow cooker with nonstick cooking spray.

4. In a large bowl, whisk together the sautéed vegetables and ¾ cup of the mozzarella cheese, the eggs, egg whites, milk, kale, and tomato. Transfer the mixture to the slow cooker.

5. Sprinkle the remaining ¼ cup cheese over the egg mixture, cover, and cook on low for 1 to 1½ hours, or until the eggs are set and a knife inserted in the center comes out clean. Serve. Season with black pepper and garnish with parsley.

Storage: When the frittata is completely cool, slice into wedges and store in an airtight container in the refrigerator for 5 to 7 days. You can eat the leftovers cold, or reheat in the oven or microwave.

PER SERVING Calories: 139; Total Fat 8g; Saturated Fat: 3g; Cholesterol: 103mg; Sodium: 185mg; Potassium: 150mg; Total Carbohydrate: 6g; Fiber: 1g; Protein: 11g

Creamy Blueberry-Banana Smoothie

Serves 2 / Prep time: 5 minutes

This heart-healthy, low-sodium smoothie is packed with ingredients that promote cardiovascular health. High-fiber oats are rich in cholesterol-lowering soluble fiber, bananas add healthy blood pressure-promoting potassium, blueberries add antioxidants, and creamy avocado and almond butter add beneficial monounsaturated fats. Filling and delicious, this quick smoothie makes a well-rounded breakfast.

1 ½ cups water (or dairy or plant-based milk of choice)
½ cup gluten-free rolled oats
1 banana, sliced and frozen
2 cups baby spinach, packed
1 cup frozen blueberries

¼ cup mashed avocado
1 cup plain nonfat Greek yogurt
½ teaspoon vanilla extract
1 tablespoon unsalted almond butter
1 cup ice

1. Add the water and oats to the base of a high-speed blender and allow the oats to soak for 2 to 3 minutes.

2. Add the banana, spinach, blueberries, avocado, yogurt, vanilla, almond butter, and ice and blend until smooth, adding more ice or water/milk until desired consistency is reached.

3. Pour into serving glasses and serve immediately.

Tip: Freeze sliced bananas in plastic bags so you have them on hand to thicken and sweeten smoothies.

Storage: Smoothies are best served immediately, but you can also store them in the refrigerator for several hours or overnight in the freezer. If stored in the fridge, there will be separation of the ingredients so stir well before enjoying.

PER SERVING Calories: 342; Total Fat 11g; Saturated Fat: 1g; Cholesterol: 0mg; Sodium: 82mg; Potassium: 461mg; Total Carbohydrate: 47g; Fiber: 9g; Protein: 18g

Overnight Spiced Oatmeal with Cranberries

Serves 2 / Prep time: 10 minutes / Chill time: 8 hours (overnight)

Overnight oats make it easy to eat a breakfast packed with nutrients, fiber, and vitamins. This delicious, heart-healthy, low-sodium oat sensation is made with just a handful of ingredients and very little prep time. Naturally sweetened, vegan, and gluten-free, you can easily double or triple the recipe and it gets better the longer it sits.

1 cup unsweetened vanilla
   almond milk
1 cup gluten-free rolled oats
¼ cup unsweetened cranberries
2 tablespoons chia seeds (optional)
¼ teaspoon cardamom

¼ teaspoon ground cinnamon
¼ teaspoon ground ginger
¼ teaspoon ground nutmeg
¼ teaspoon vanilla extract
Optional toppings: sliced almonds,
   additional cranberries

1. In a medium bowl, combine the almond milk, oats, cranberries, chia seeds (if using), cardamom, cinnamon, ginger, nutmeg, and vanilla extract. Cover the bowl with plastic wrap and refrigerate for 8 hours and up to overnight.

2. Before serving, stir thoroughly, portion into serving bowls, and top with sliced almonds and more cranberries if desired.

Tip: Add-ins are the best part of morning oats. Use your favorite nuts; fresh, frozen, or dried fruits; stir in yogurt or ricotta; or some honey or maple syrup.

Storage: Overnight oats can be stored in the refrigerator for up to 5 days.

PER SERVING Calories: 220; Total Fat 4g; Saturated Fat: 0g; Cholesterol: 0mg; Sodium: 75mg; Potassium: 89mg; Total Carbohydrate: 40g; Fiber: 5g; Protein: 6g

Overnight Oatmeal with Banana and Chocolate

Serves 1 / Prep time: 5 minutes / Chill Time: 8 hours (overnight)

I love the versatility of overnight oats. There are so many different options for flavors from sweet to savory, plus it is a great time saver if your mornings tend to be rushed. The oats can also be heated on a cold day or served cold. (This recipe is adapted from OrganizeYourselfSkinny.com)

½ cup gluten-free rolled oats
½ tablespoon cocoa powder
1 teaspoon milk chocolate morsels
⅛ teaspoon cinnamon
¼ teaspoon pure vanilla extract

½ cup unsweetened coconut milk, plus more as needed
½ banana peeled and chopped
1 to 2 teaspoons pure maple syrup

1. In a pint-size mason jar, combine the rolled oats, cocoa powder, chocolate morsels, and cinnamon.

2. Stir in the vanilla extract, coconut milk, banana, and maple syrup.

3. Cover and refrigerate 8 hours, or up to overnight.

4. Before serving, stir thoroughly. Add a little more coconut milk if needed, to loosen it up and to get the consistency you want.

PER SERVING Calories: 297; Total Fat 7g; Saturated Fat: 3g; Cholesterol: 1mg; Sodium: 4mg; Potassium: 306mg; Total Carbohydrate: 56g; Fiber: 7g; Protein: 6g

Honey-Lime Quinoa Fruit Salad

Serves 4 / Prep time: 5 minutes / Cook time: 15 minutes

SODIUM

LOWEST

MEATLESS
DAIRY-FREE
GLUTEN-FREE
LOW-FAT

Mix up your morning routine by having a sweet and colorful bowl of nutritious berries and power-packed quinoa dressed with a honey-lime glaze. Quinoa and berries are delicious and nutritious.

FOR THE FRUIT SALAD

1 cup uncooked quinoa

1 cup sliced blackberries

1 cup sliced strawberries

1 cup sliced blueberries

1 mango, diced

1 kiwi, sliced

1 tablespoon chopped fresh mint, for garnish

FOR THE GLAZE

¼ cup honey

2 tablespoons freshly squeezed lime juice

1 tablespoon chia seeds (optional)

2 to 3 tablespoons water

TO MAKE THE FRUIT SALAD

1. Rinse and prepare the quinoa according to package directions. Cool the quinoa to room temperature.

2. In a large bowl, combine the quinoa, blackberries, blueberries, strawberries, mango, and kiwi.

TO MAKE THE GLAZE

In a small bowl combine the honey, lime juice, chia seeds (if using), and water. Drizzle the glaze over the fruit salad and toss to coat. Garnish with the fresh mint.

Storage: Store the fruit salad in an airtight container in the refrigerator for 1 to 2 days.

PER SERVING Calories: 321; Total Fat 3g; Saturated Fat: 0g; Cholesterol: 0mg; Sodium: 15mg; Potassium: 321mg; Total Carbohydrate: 71g; Fiber: 8g; Protein: 7g

Orange-Almond Muffins

Makes 6 muffins / Prep time: 15 minutes / Cook time: 20 to 22 minutes

Orange plus almonds is a no-fail combination and this recipe puts the emphasis on health, with the use of whole-grain oat flour and vitamin E–rich wheat germ. Greek yogurt and eggs keep them moist and fluffy, with sweetness provided by mashed banana and a dash of brown sugar.

1 large egg, separated

1 teaspoon extra-virgin olive oil

2 tablespoons nonfat Greek yogurt

2 teaspoons almond extract

1 ½ cups gluten-free oat flour

2 tablespoons wheat germ

1 teaspoon baking powder

½ teaspoon baking soda

1 teaspoon orange zest

½ cup slivered blanched almonds, divided

¼ cup low-fat buttermilk

⅓ cup orange juice

2 teaspoons light brown sugar

1. Preheat the oven to 375°F.

2. In a medium bowl, beat the egg yolk with a whisk until frothy. Add the olive oil and whisk some more. Add the Greek yogurt and almond extract while whisking.

3. In another medium bowl, mix together the oat flour, wheat germ, baking powder, baking soda, orange zest, and ¼ cup of the almonds.

4. Gently fold the egg yolk mixture into the flour mixture.

5. In another medium bowl, whisk the egg whites until frothy and white. Fold it into the muffin batter.

6. Slowly add the buttermilk and orange juice, gently mixing after each addition until smooth.

7. Line a standard-size muffin tin with 6 paper liners and fill each liner with an equal amount of the batter. Sprinkle the top with the brown sugar and the remaining ¼ cup almonds.

8. Bake for 20 to 22 minutes or until a toothpick inserted in the center comes out clean.

Tip: If you like your muffins on the sweeter side but want to keep them low in added sugar, add ½ cup granulated stevia.

Storage: The muffins will keep for 3 to 5 days stored in a plastic bag in the refrigerator. These also freeze well for up to a month if sealed tightly in a plastic freezer bag.

PER SERVING (1 muffin) Calories: 208; Total Fat 7g; Saturated Fat: 1g; Cholesterol: 32mg; Sodium: 211mg; Potassium: 142mg; Total Carbohydrate: 30g; Fiber: 6g; Protein: 7g

Avocado Toast with Basil Pesto

Serves 2 / Prep time: 10 minutes

This quick and easy recipe pumps up the flavor with fresh basil, lemon, and pepper. You won't miss the salt. Rich in heart-healthy monounsaturated fats from walnuts and avocado, this simple but classic recipe is a great choice when you can't decide what to make for breakfast.

FOR THE PESTO

⅓ cup fresh basil leaves, loosely packed

¼ cup walnuts

Juice of 1 lemon

⅛ teaspoon freshly ground black pepper

⅛ teaspoon garlic powder

1 tablespoon extra-virgin olive oil

1 tablespoon hot water

FOR THE TOAST

3 slices crusty whole-grain bread

1 avocado, sliced

Microgreens, for garnish

Freshly ground black pepper

Extra-virgin olive oil (optional)

Lemon wedges (optional)

TO MAKE THE PESTO

Add the basil, walnuts, lemon juice, black pepper, garlic powder, olive oil, and water to a blender or food processor. Blend until smooth, with some nut pieces remaining for texture.

TO MAKE THE TOAST

1. Toast the bread.

2. Divide the avocado slices equally among the toast slices.

3. Spread 2 tablespoons of the pesto over the avocado. Add the microgreens to garnish and season with black pepper.

4. Drizzle with additional olive oil and lemon juice (if using), and serve immediately.

Tip: To save time, prepare the pesto the night before and store in a covered container in the refrigerator.

Storage: The pesto will keep in the fridge for 2 to 3 days stored in an airtight container.

PER SERVING Calories: 396; Total Fat 32g; Saturated Fat: 4g; Cholesterol:0 mg; Sodium: 201mg; Potassium: 538mg; Total Carbohydrate: 27g; Fiber: 10g; Protein: 10g

Chorizo Sweet Potato Hash

Serves 8 / Prep time: 15 minutes / Cook time: 35 to 45 minutes

I'm a fan of the savory side of breakfast items. Hash is not just limited to being a breakfast item—I've been known to make a quick hash for dinner, especially because most of the ingredients are in my pantry at any time.

FOR THE SAUSAGE

1 tablespoon ground cumin

1 tablespoon sodium-free garlic powder

1 tablespoon sodium-free onion powder

1 tablespoon pimentón (Spanish paprika)

1 teaspoon freshly ground black pepper

1 teaspoon sodium-free chili pepper

1 teaspoon ground cloves

1 teaspoon ground coriander

1 teaspoon dried thyme

½ teaspoon cayenne pepper

1 pound low-sodium ground pork

2 tablespoons cider vinegar

Zest of 1 lime

FOR THE HASH

1-pound container fresh baby or mature Brussels sprouts (or 1 package frozen)

2 Granny Smith apples, cored and cubed

2 large sweet potatoes, peeled and cubed

1 medium zucchini, peeled, seeded, and cubed.

1 medium yellow onion, diced

2 tablespoons extra-virgin olive oil

FOR THE GLAZE

¼ cup pure maple syrup

2 tablespoons extra-virgin olive oil

2 tablespoons balsamic vinegar

1 tablespoon chipotle pepper

Freshly ground black pepper

TO MAKE THE SAUSAGE

1. In a mortar and pestle or a grinder (I use a coffee bean grinder), grind together the cumin, garlic powder, onion powder, pimentón, black pepper, chili pepper, cloves, coriander, thyme, and cayenne.

2. In large bowl, mix together the ground spices, pork, vinegar, and lime zest.

3. Let the sausage sit in the refrigerator for 10 to 20 minutes before cooking to let the spices meld. If desired, divide it into 8 small balls and form patties.

TO MAKE THE HASH

1. Meanwhile, prepare the hash. Preheat the oven (or a grill) to 400°F. Line a large baking sheet or roasting pan with foil and generously grease with olive oil.

2. If using mature Brussels sprouts, remove any tough outer leaves cut them in half. Leave frozen or baby Brussels sprouts whole. Transfer to a large bowl.

3. Add the apples, sweet potatoes, zucchini, and onions, and drizzle with olive oil.

TO MAKE THE GLAZE

1. Mix together the maple syrup, olive oil, vinegar, chipotle pepper, and season with black pepper.

2. Toss the glaze with the vegetables and spread them out in one layer on the prepared baking sheet. Bake until sweet potatoes are tender and Brussels sprouts are lightly browned, 25 to 30 minutes.

3. Mix in the chorizo and return to the oven to bake another 10 to 15 minutes. Once the vegetables are cooked through, toss and serve.

PER SERVING Calories: 341; Total Fat 20g; Saturated Fat: 6g; Cholesterol:41 mg; Sodium: 58mg; Potassium: 660mg; Total Carbohydrate: 31g; Fiber: 6g; Protein: 13g

Traditional Hummus p.78

6

SNACKS AND SIDES

MEATLESS
GLUTEN-FREE
LOW-FAT
ONE-POT

Slow-Cooker Garlic Cauliflower Mashed "Potatoes"

Serves 6 / Prep time: 5 minutes / Cook time: 2 to 3 hours on high, 4 to 6 hours on low

This nutritious recipe gives you the feeling you are eating mashed potatoes with a fraction of the calories and carbohydrates. High in fiber, vitamin C, and disease-protective phytochemicals, this healthy side dish goes great with grilled chicken or fish. Serve it anywhere you would use mashed potatoes.

1 head of cauliflower

3 cups water

4 garlic cloves

1 shallot

1 bay leaf

1 tablespoon extra-virgin olive oil

1 to 2 tablespoons milk

Freshly ground black pepper

¼ cup minced chives, for garnish

1. Cut the cauliflower into florets and place them in the slow cooker.

2. Add the water, garlic, shallot, and bay leaf.

3. Cover and cook on high for 2 to 3 hours, or on low for 4 to 6 hours.

4. Drain the water. Remove and discard the garlic cloves, shallot, and bay leaf.

5. Mix in the olive oil.

6. Using a potato masher, mash the cauliflower, or use an immersion blender to make it creamier. Add the milk, a little at a time, until the desired consistency is reached.

7. Season with black pepper, and serve topped with chives.

Cooking Tip: If you are short on time use 3 to 4 cups of prewashed, precut cauliflower florets.

Storage: Store the mashed cauliflower in an airtight, covered container in the refrigerator for 3 to 5 days. Mashed cauliflower freezes well and heats up quickly. Freeze in heavy-duty freezer bags for up to 10 months.

PER SERVING Calories: 51; Total Fat 3g; Saturated Fat: 0g; Cholesterol: 0mg; Sodium: 45mg; Potassium: 314mg; Total Carbohydrate: 6g; Fiber: 3g; Protein: 2g

Slow-Cooker Cranberry-Balsamic Brussels Sprouts

Serves 4 / Prep time: 10 minutes
Cook time: 2 hours and 15 minutes on high, 4 hours and 30 minutes on low

High in cholesterol-lowering fiber, antioxidants, and vitamins and minerals, slow-cooking Brussels sprouts brings out their sweet, nutty flavor, while diminishing their characteristic bitterness. Drizzled with a balsamic reduction, this tasty side dish goes with most savory entrees.

1 tablespoon stone-
   ground mustard
1 tablespoon extra-virgin olive oil
¼ cup water
1 pound Brussels sprouts, trimmed
   and halved

4 garlic cloves
⅓ cup dried cranberries, chopped
⅛ teaspoon freshly ground
   black pepper
Pinch paprika
½ cup balsamic vinegar

1. In a medium bowl, combine and thoroughly whisk the mustard, olive oil, and water.

2. In a slow cooker, place the Brussels sprouts, garlic, and dried cranberries. Add the mustard dressing and stir to coat. Season with the salt, black pepper, and paprika.

3. Cook on high for 2 hours and 15 minutes or on low for 4½ hours, or until the sprouts are tender and lightly browned.

4. Add the vinegar to a small pot, and bring to a boil. Reduce to a simmer and cook, stirring frequently, until it thickens to a syrup-like consistency, about 12 minutes.

5. Stir the sprouts and drizzle with the balsamic reduction. Serve immediately.

Storage: The cooked Brussels sprouts will keep in the refrigerator, stored in an airtight container, for 3 to 5 days. You can also freeze them in heavy-duty freezer bags for up to 10 months.

PER SERVING Calories: 130; Total Fat 4g; Saturated Fat: 1g; Cholesterol: 0mg; Sodium: 79mg; Potassium: 459mg; Total Carbohydrate: 23g; Fiber: 5g; Protein: 4g

Slow-Cooker Glazed Carrots and Peppers

Serves 7 / Prep time: 15 minutes
Cook time: 3 to 4 hours on high, 7 to 8 hours on low, plus 15 minutes to rest

Carrots are high in beta-carotene and fiber and can help reduce the risk of heart disease. Slow-cooked and topped with a sweet and spicy glaze, this colorful and delicious side dish works well with grilled chicken or fish.

¼ cup low-sugar apricot preserves

2 tablespoons brown sugar

1 tablespoon light whipped butter

1 teaspoon cinnamon

¼ teaspoon ground nutmeg

2 pounds carrots, peeled and chopped

1 red onion, sliced

1 yellow bell pepper, seeded and sliced

1 green pepper, stem removed, seeded, and sliced

1 tablespoon cornstarch

2 tablespoons cold water

1. In a small bowl, stir together the preserves, brown sugar, butter, cinnamon, and nutmeg. Add the carrots, onion, and bell peppers to the slow cooker. Add the glaze and stir to coat.

2. Cover and cook on low for 7 to 8 hours, or on high for 3 to 4 hours.

3. When the vegetables are cooked, in another small bowl, combine the cornstarch and the water, and stir until the cornstarch has dissolved. Add the slurry to the slow cooker and mix well.

4. Turn off the slow cooker and leave uncovered until the sauce has thickened, about 15 minutes. Stir and enjoy.

Tip: You can replace the bell peppers with other root vegetables such as parsnips and add optional seasonings including black pepper, ground ginger, and cayenne pepper.

PER SERVING Calories: 114; Total Fat 1g; Saturated Fat: 0g; Cholesterol: 1mg; Sodium: 98mg; Potassium: 529mg; Total Carbohydrate: 26g; Fiber: 5g; Protein: 2g

Slow-Cooker Spiced Nuts

Makes 8 cups / Prep time: 5 minutes / Cook time: 1 hour 30 minutes

SODIUM

LOWEST

MEATLESS
DAIRY-FREE
GLUTEN-FREE
ONE-POT

Made in the slow cooker, this sweet and spicy nut mix makes a nutritious snack high in heart-healthy omega-3 and monounsaturated fats. Sprinkle the nuts over roasted pears or apples, add them to a cheese, vegetable, and hummus plate, or simply eat them as a healthy snack.

4 cups raw, unsalted mixed nuts
   (almonds, cashews, pecans, etc.)

1 teaspoon ground cinnamon

¼ teaspoon ground ginger

¼ teaspoon ground nutmeg

⅓ cup pure maple syrup

1 teaspoon vanilla extract

Zest of 1 orange

1. In a medium bowl, combine the nuts, cinnamon, ginger, and nutmeg.

2. Add the maple syrup, vanilla, and orange zest and toss thoroughly to coat.

3. Spray the inside of a slow cooker with nonstick spray. Add the spiced nut mixture. Cover and cook on low for 1½ hours, stirring every 15 minutes.

4. Turn off the slow cooker and spread the nuts onto waxed paper to cool completely.

Storage: Store the nuts in an airtight container for up to 1 week or in heavy-duty freezer bags in the freezer for up to 12 months.

PER SERVING (½ cup) Calories: 357; Total Fat 28g; Saturated Fat: 3g; Cholesterol: 0mg; Sodium: 1mg; Potassium: 30mg; Total Carbohydrate: 23g; Fiber: 4g; Protein: 10g

Kale Chips

Serves 2 / Prep time: 5 minutes / Cook time: 25 minutes

Homemade kale chips are a nutritious alternative to salty corn or potato chips. Easily found in most grocery stores, kale is low in calories, high in cholesterol-lowering fiber, high in the antioxidant vitamins A and C, and a good source of heart-healthy, anti-inflammatory omega-3 fatty acids. These chips are quick to prepare and are seasoned with garlic powder in place of salt making them a great fit for a low-sodium diet.

12 flat-leaf kale leaves, stems removed

Cooking spray

Salt-free garlic powder

Freshly ground black pepper

1. Preheat the oven to 300°F.

2. Using scissors, cut up the kale leaves into pieces about 2 inches square.

3. Place the kale pieces in a single layer on a large nonstick baking sheet. Do not overlap.

4. Very lightly mist the leaves with the cooking spray, then season with garlic powder and black pepper.

5. Bake for 10 minutes, then rotate the pan and bake for 15 minutes more.

6. Allow to cool for about 3 minutes before enjoying.

Tip: Avoid adding liquid seasonings like hot sauce or vinegar as liquids can result in soggy chips.

Storage: Kale chips are best eaten the same day they are made, as they tend to wilt and get soggy over time. If you need to store them, place dry, uncooked rice into the bottom of an airtight storage container then put the kale chips loosely on top. Eat within 1 to 2 days.

PER SERVING Calories: 37; Total Fat 1g; Saturated Fat: 0g; Cholesterol: 0mg; Sodium: 30mg; Potassium: 299mg; Total Carbohydrate: 8g; Fiber: 3g; Protein: 3g

Simple Roasted Chickpeas

Serves 4 / Prep time: 10 minutes / Cook time: 40 to 45 minutes

Oven-roasted chickpeas are about as simple as it gets, and they make a healthy snack to satisfy a craving for something crunchy. Slightly addictive, this recipe uses four ingredients and starts with a can of chickpeas you may already have in your pantry. Tasty on their own, roasted chickpeas also make a great salad topper.

1½ tablespoons extra-virgin olive oil

2 to 4 teaspoons spices or finely chopped herbs like chili powder, garlic powder, curry powder, freshly ground black pepper, smoked paprika, chives, parsley, cilantro, dill

1 (15-ounce) can garbanzo beans (chickpeas), drained and rinsed

1. Preheat the oven to 350°F.

2. In a small bowl, whisk the oil and seasonings together, then add the chickpeas and toss to coat. Spread on a baking sheet in a single layer.

3. Roast in the preheated oven, stirring occasionally, until nicely browned and slightly crispy, 40 to 45 minutes.

Tip: For best results, ensure your beans are allowed to drain thoroughly. If you have the time, spread the beans on a paper towel, cover them with another towel, and gently press to absorb any remaining water.

Storage: Roasted chickpeas can be stored in an airtight container for up to a week. It is not recommended to freeze roasted chickpeas as this will alter their texture.

PER SERVING Calories: 142; Total Fat 5g; Saturated Fat: 1g; Cholesterol: 0mg; Sodium: 1mg; Potassium: 17mg; Total Carbohydrate: 18g; Fiber: 5g; Protein: 6g

Traditional Hummus

Makes 1½ cups / Prep time: 10 minutes

A traditional Middle Eastern dip, hummus is quickly prepared using a handful of simple ingredients you might already have on hand in your pantry. Homemade hummus is much lower in sodium than most premade brands and tastes better too. Use as a dip for freshly cut vegetables or a healthy sandwich spread.

¼ cup tahini, well-stirred

¼ cup freshly squeezed lemon juice

2 tablespoons extra-virgin olive oil, plus additional for garnish

2 small garlic cloves, minced

1 teaspoon cumin

⊠ teaspoon freshly ground black pepper

1 (15-ounce) can garbanzo beans (chickpeas), drained and rinsed

2 to 3 tablespoons water

½ teaspoon ground paprika, for garnish

1. In the bowl of a food processor, combine the tahini and lemon juice and process for 1 minute. Scrape down the sides and bottom of the bowl, then process for 30 seconds more.

2. Add the olive oil, garlic, cumin, and black pepper to the food processor and process for 30 seconds. Scrape down the sides and bottom of the bowl then process until well blended, or 30 seconds.

3. Add half of the chickpeas to the food processor and process for 1 minute. Scrape down the sides and bottom of the bowl, then add the remaining chickpeas and process until thick and quite smooth, 1 to 2 minutes.

4. If the hummus is too thick, slowly add 2 to 3 tablespoons of water with the food processor running, until the desired consistency is reached.

5. Serve with a drizzle of olive oil and paprika.

Tip: This is a basic recipe for hummus that you can mix up by adding ingredients like roasted red peppers, sun-dried tomatoes, or salt-free spice mixes.

Storage: Store homemade hummus in an airtight container and refrigerate for up to 1 week. It is not recommended to freeze hummus as the taste and texture will be altered.

PER SERVING (¼ cup) Calories: 168; Total Fat 10g; Saturated Fat: 1g; Cholesterol: 0mg; Sodium: 12mg; Potassium: 62mg; Total Carbohydrate: 15g; Fiber: 4g; Protein: 6g

Oven-Roasted Vegetables with Rosemary

Serves 8 / Prep time: 20 minutes / Cook time: 40 to 45 minutes

The naturally sweet flavors that come from oven-roasted golden brown veggies gives them a mouthwatering taste that is hard to resist. Wonderfully tender, flavored with rosemary, and seasoned to perfection, this dish is the perfect accompaniment to any meal.

Cooking spray

1 pound Yukon gold potatoes, cut into 1-inch pieces

4 carrots, peeled and cut into 1-inch pieces

4 medium zucchini, cut into 1-inch pieces

1 red bell pepper, cut into 1-inch pieces

1 large Vidalia onion, cut into 1-inch pieces

6 to 8 garlic cloves

3 tablespoons extra-virgin olive oil, divided

½ teaspoon freshly ground black pepper, divided

2 tablespoons chopped fresh rosemary, divided

2 medium beets, peeled and cut into 1-inch pieces

2 sprigs fresh rosemary, for garnish (optional)

1. Preheat the oven to 400°F, with oven racks placed in the two bottom positions. Lightly coat two baking sheets with the cooking spray.

2. In a large bowl, stir together the potatoes, carrots, zucchini, bell pepper, onion, and garlic. Drizzle 2 tablespoons of the olive oil and season with ¼ teaspoon of the black pepper, and 1½ tablespoons of the chopped rosemary. Stir to combine.

3. Place beets in a medium bowl. Drizzle the remaining 1 tablespoon olive oil over the beets and season with the remaining ¼ teaspoon black pepper and ½ tablespoon chopped rosemary. Stir to combine.

4. Divide the vegetables evenly between the two prepared baking sheets. Roast for 20 minutes, then gently stir the vegetables and rotate the baking sheets from rack to rack and front to back. Roast until the vegetables are tender when pierced with a fork and golden brown in some spots, 20 to 25 minutes more.

5. Serve garnished with the rosemary sprigs (if using).

Tip: Using two baking sheets gives the vegetables enough room to allow them to truly roast and brown, rather than steam.

Storage: Store in an airtight container in the refrigerator for 3 to 5 days. Reheat in the oven at 425°F for 15 to 20 minutes.

PER SERVING Calories: 135; Total Fat 6g; Saturated Fat: 1g; Cholesterol: 0mg; Sodium: 29mg; Potassium: 707mg; Total Carbohydrate: 22g; Fiber: 4g; Protein: 3g

Mexican Street Corn with Chipotle Mayo

Serves: 4 / Prep time: 5 minutes / Cook time: 6 to 10 minutes

I first encountered Mexican-style sweet corn while living in Florida. I used my grill daily, and corn on the cob is easy to grill. It makes a great side dish for almost any meal. You can control the tartness in the recipe by adding more or less lime.

4 ears husked sweet corn

2 tablespoons corn oil

½ cup low-sodium mayonnaise

1 teaspoon chili powder

1 teaspoon garlic powder

½ teaspoon chipotle powder

Freshly ground black pepper

1 lime, quartered

1. Preheat a grill pan.

2. Brush the corn with the oil and place on the grill pan.

3. Grill, turning corn, so all sides are charred, 6 to 10 minutes.

4. Meanwhile, stir together the mayonnaise, chili powder, garlic powder, chipotle powder, and black pepper.

5. Remove the corn from the grill and brush with the chipotle mayo.

6. Serve with lime quarters to squeeze over the corn.

PER SERVING Calories: 327; Total Fat 28g; Saturated Fat: 4g; Cholesterol: 8mg; Sodium: 161mg; Potassium: 283mg; Total Carbohydrate: 20g; Fiber: 3g; Protein: 3g

Grilled Pineapple with Caramel Bourbon Glaze

SODIUM

LOWEST

Serves 6 / Prep time: 10 minutes / Cook time: 6 to 10 minutes

I love cooked pineapple. It's a great way to brighten up any dish and works well with Latin, Asian, and Caribbean cuisine. The Bourbon glaze turns the pineapple into candy in this preparation. My kids love it over coconut rice or vanilla ice cream. This recipe is adapted from allrecipes.com.

MEATLESS
DAIRY-FREE
GLUTEN-FREE
LOW-FAT

1 cup brown sugar

2 teaspoons ground cinnamon

1 ounce bourbon (optional)

1 pineapple peeled, cored, and cut into wedges

1. Preheat an outdoor grill to medium-high and lightly oil the grate.

2. Whisk the brown sugar and cinnamon together in a bowl.

3. Pour the sugar mixture into a large resealable plastic bag, and add the bourbon and pineapple wedges. Shake to coat each wedge.

4. Grill the pineapple wedges until heated through, 3 to 5 minutes per side.

PER SERVING Calories: 132; Total Fat 0g; Saturated Fat: 0g; Cholesterol: 0mg; Sodium: 11mg; Potassium: 177mg; Total Carbohydrate: 43g; Fiber: 1g; Protein: 0g

Slow-Cooker Turkey Chili p.94

7

SALADS AND SOUPS

Slow-Cooker Moroccan Lentil Soup

SODIUM

LOWER

MEATLESS
DAIRY-FREE
GLUTEN-FREE
LOW-FAT
ONE-POT

Serves 8 / Prep time: 15 minutes / Cook time: 4 to 5 hours on high, 8 to 10 hours on low

This delicious Moroccan-inspired soup is full of plant-powered protein from nutrient-rich lentils. Lentils are sodium-free and a good source of cholesterol-lowering fiber and heart-healthy vitamins, minerals, and antioxidants. Richly seasoned with Middle Eastern spices, serve this soup with hummus and pita bread.

2 cups chopped onion

2 cups chopped carrot

1 cup chopped bell pepper

4 garlic cloves, minced

2 teaspoons extra-virgin olive oil

1 teaspoon ground coriander

1 teaspoon ground cumin

1 teaspoon ground turmeric

¼ teaspoon ground cinnamon

¼ teaspoon freshly ground
   black pepper

6 cups low-sodium vegetable broth

2 cups water

3 cups chopped cauliflower

1¾ cups dry lentils

1 (28-ounce) can no-salt
   diced tomatoes

4 cups chopped fresh spinach,
   or 1 (10-ounce) package frozen
   chopped spinach, thawed

2 tablespoons freshly squeezed
   lemon juice

Chopped cilantro, for garnish
   (optional)

1. Combine the onion, carrot, bell pepper, garlic, olive oil, coriander, cumin, turmeric, cinnamon, and black pepper in a slow cooker. Add the broth, water, cauliflower, lentils, and tomatoes, and stir until well combined.

2. Cover and cook until lentils are tender, 4 to 5 hours on high, or 8 to 10 hours on low.

3. During the last 30 minutes of cooking, stir in the spinach. Just before serving stir in the lemon juice.

4. Garnish with chopped cilantro (if using).

Tip: For easy clean up, try a slow-cooker liner. These heat-resistant, disposable liners fit neatly in the insert and help prevent food from sticking to the bottom and sides of your slow cooker.

Storage: Cover and refrigerate for up to 3 days or freeze for up to 6 months. Stir in the lemon juice and optional cilantro just before serving.

PER SERVING Calories: 150; Total Fat 2g; Saturated Fat: 0g; Cholesterol: 0mg; Sodium: 194mg; Potassium: 400mg; Total Carbohydrate: 34g; Fiber: 13g; Protein: 8g

Slow-Cooker Minestrone Soup

SODIUM

LOWER

MEATLESS
DAIRY-FREE
LOW-FAT
ONE-POT

Serves 8 / Prep time: 5 minutes
Cook time: 8 to 10 hours on high, 4 to 5 hours on low, plus 10 to 20 minutes for the pasta

Minestrone soup is a thick soup of Italian origin loaded with nutritious vegetables and protein-rich beans. Hearty and healthy, minestrone lacks a "fixed" recipe so you will see many recipes with a wide variation in ingredients. This slow-cooker version uses many traditional ingredients including whole wheat pasta.

1 cup diced celery

1 cup diced carrot

1 cup diced onion

1 cup fresh green beans, cut into 1-inch pieces

64-ounces low-sodium vegetable broth

2 (14.5-ounce) cans no-salt diced tomatoes

1 (15-ounce) can kidney beans, drained and rinsed

1 (15-ounce) can great northern beans, drained and rinsed

4 garlic cloves, minced

1 tablespoon dried basil

2 teaspoons dried oregano

2 teaspoons dried thyme

½ teaspoon dried rosemary, crushed

1 bay leaf

1 teaspoon freshly ground black pepper

1½ cups dried whole wheat elbow pasta

1. Add all of the ingredients except the pasta to a slow cooker. Cook for 8 to 10 hours, or on high for 4 to 5 hours. Adjust seasonings.

2. Just before serving, turn slow cooker to high (if you had been cooking on low), and cook for about 10 minutes. Add the pasta and cook until pasta is al dente, 10 to 20 minutes. Serve immediately.

Tip: This soup is highly customizable so add your favorite fresh or frozen vegetables and canned beans.

Storage: If you plan on storing the soup, cook the pasta separately and add to the soup before serving. Otherwise the pasta will continue to absorb liquid and get soggy. Store in an airtight container in the refrigerator for 3 to 4 days. You can also freeze in freezer safe airtight containers for 4 to 6 months.

PER SERVING Calories: 216; Total Fat 1g; Saturated Fat: 0g; Cholesterol: 0mg; Sodium: 166mg; Potassium: 254mg; Total Carbohydrate: 42g; Fiber: 9g; Protein: 10g

SODIUM

LOWEST

MEATLESS
DAIRY-FREE
GLUTEN-FREE
LOW-FAT
ONE-POT

Slow-Cooker Black Bean Soup

Serves 8 / Prep time: 5 minutes / Cook time: 4 hours on high, 8 hours on low

This effortless, time saving black bean soup recipe is made with just a few simple pantry ingredients to create a flavorful nourishing soup. Brightly seasoned with cilantro and added peppers, the sodium content is kept low by using a mix of water and low-sodium vegetable broth.

1 tablespoon extra-virgin olive oil

1 medium yellow onion, chopped

1 red bell pepper, chopped

1 yellow bell pepper, chopped

4 garlic cloves, minced

4 (15-ounce) cans black beans, drained and rinsed

4 cups water

4 cups low-sodium vegetable broth

1 teaspoon ground cumin

¾ teaspoon freshly ground black pepper

½ cup chopped fresh cilantro

Juice of 1 lime, optional

1. In a large skillet over medium-high heat, heat the olive oil. Add the onion and bell peppers and sauté until the onion is translucent, 4 to 5 minutes. Add the garlic and cook until the garlic is fragrant, about 1 minute.

2. Pour the black beans into the slow cooker, then add the onion and pepper mixture. Add the water, broth, cumin, and black pepper. Stir to combine the ingredients. Cook for 8 hours on low, or 4 hours on high.

3. Once the soup is done, stir in the cilantro and lime juice (if using). Serve warm.

Tip: You could also use dry beans for this recipe. Soak 1 pound of black beans for 8 to 12 hours (overnight) in 6 cups of water. Discard the soaking water and add the soaked beans to the slow cooker in place of the canned beans.

Storage: Store the cooked soup in the refrigerator in a covered container for 3 to 4 days. You can also freeze the soup in airtight containers for 4 to 6 months.

PER SERVING Calories: 236; Total Fat 2g; Saturated Fat: 0g; Cholesterol: 0mg; Sodium: 72mg; Potassium: 129mg; Total Carbohydrate: 41g; Fiber: 10g; Protein: 13g

Slow-Cooker Chicken Noodle Soup

Serves 6 / Prep time: 15 minutes / Cook time: 6 to 7 hours on low, plus 10 minutes to rest

A classic comfort food, this recipe for slow-cooker chicken noodle soup is full of lean, high-quality protein and nutritious vegetables. Hearty and comforting, this soup is perfect for a cold winter day or for fighting off a flu.

1 ½ pounds boneless, skinless chicken breasts

6 medium carrots, peeled and thinly sliced (about 2 cups)

1 medium yellow onion, finely chopped

4 stalks celery, thinly chopped

4 garlic cloves, minced

2 tablespoons extra-virgin olive oil

6 cups low-sodium chicken broth

1 cup water

1 teaspoon dried thyme

½ teaspoon dried rosemary, crushed

½ teaspoon dried sage

¼ teaspoon celery seed, finely crushed

2 bay leaves

Freshly ground black pepper

2 cups uncooked wide egg noodles

¼ cup chopped fresh parsley

1. Add the chicken, carrots, onion, celery, and garlic to a slow cooker. Drizzle the olive oil over the vegetables, then add in chicken broth, water, thyme, rosemary, sage, celery seed, bay leaves, and black pepper.

2. Cover and cook on low heat for 6 to7 hours.

3. Remove the cooked chicken and allow to rest for 10 minutes, then dice into bite size pieces. Meanwhile add the egg noodles and parsley to the slow cooker. Increase the temperature to high, cover, and cook until noodles are tender, or 10 minutes. Return the diced chicken to the slow cooker and mix in. Serve warm.

Storage: Chicken noodle soup will keep in the refrigerator in an airtight container for 3 to 4 days. You can also freeze leftovers in airtight containers for 4 to 6 months.

PER SERVING Calories: 289; Total Fat 10g; Saturated Fat: 2g; Cholesterol: 79mg; Sodium: 195mg; Potassium: 398mg; Total Carbohydrate: 20g; Fiber: 4g; Protein: 30g

Slow-Cooker Butternut Squash Soup

Serves 4 / Prep time: 15 minutes / Cook time: 4 hours on high, 8 hours on low

This easy, creamy recipe for butternut squash soup cuts down on prep time by eliminating the need to peel the squash. Loaded with fiber and the antioxidants beta-carotene and vitamin A, this vegan, gluten-free recipe is low in sodium yet full of flavor.

1 (32-ounce) butternut squash, halved and seeded (about 4 cups)
2 large shallots, quartered
2 garlic cloves, minced
2 cups low-sodium vegetable broth

¾ cup light coconut milk
⅛ teaspoon freshly ground black pepper
Pinch nutmeg
Chopped chives, for garnish (optional)

1. Place the squash, shallots, garlic, and broth in a slow cooker.

2. Cook on low for 8 hours, or on high 4 hours, until the squash is soft and a knife can easily be inserted.

3. Remove the squash from its skin and discard the peel.

4. Stir in the coconut milk, black pepper, and nutmeg.

5. Transfer the mixture to a blender or use an immersion blender to blend until smooth.

6. Serve garnished with chives (if using).

Tip: You could substitute the butternut squash for an equal weight of either buttercup or Kabocha squash, or use a combination of your favorite squash.

Storage: Store the cooked soup in the refrigerator in airtight containers for 3 to 4 days or in the freezer in airtight containers for 4 to 6 months.

PER SERVING Calories: 124; Total Fat 3g; Saturated Fat: 2g; Cholesterol: 0mg; Sodium: 100mg; Potassium: 605mg; Total Carbohydrate: 25g; Fiber: 7g; Protein: 3g

Slow-Cooker Tortilla Chicken Soup

Serves 6 / Prep time: 15 minutes / Cook time 6 to 8 hours on low

Tortilla chicken soup is easily one of my most favorite soups. This is my go-to food if I'm feeling run-down. The spices help clear the sinuses more than chicken noodle soup. I've also served this soup over rice to make it a more filling meal.

Cooking spray

1½ pounds boneless, skinless chicken thighs

2 cups frozen Southwest mixed vegetables (corn, black beans, red peppers)

1 (10-ounce) can Ro-Tel® or Del Monte® no-salt-added diced tomatoes and green chilies, undrained

1 tablespoon ground chipotle chili pepper

1½ teaspoons ground cumin

4 cups no-salt-added chicken broth

¼ cup freshly squeezed lime juice

Tortilla strips, diced avocado, chopped cilantro, for garnish (optional)

1. Spray the inner pot of a slow cooker with cooking spray.

2. Add the chicken, frozen vegetables, undrained tomatoes, chipotle pepper, cumin, and broth to the slow cooker.

3. Cover and cook on low 6 to 8 hours or until the chicken is tender.

4. Remove the chicken from the slow cooker and shred it using 2 forks.

5. Return the chicken to the slow cooker. Stir in the lime juice.

6. Serve topped with tortilla strips, avocado, and cilantro (if using).

PER SERVING Calories: 197; Total Fat 4g; Saturated Fat: 2g; Cholesterol: 65mg; Sodium: 175mg; Potassium: 160mg; Total Carbohydrate: 10g; Fiber: 2g; Protein: 30g

Slow-Cooker Turkey Chili

Serves 4 / Prep time: 15 minutes / Cook time: 4 to 5 hours on high, 6 to 8 hours on low

Slow-cooker chili is a staple in our house, whether it's for tailgating at a game or just as a comfort meal. This chili has all the flavor and none of the salt of canned chili, and you can control the heat depending on your palate.

FOR THE CHILI SEASONING

½ cup chili powder

¼ cup garlic powder

¼ cup cumin

3 tablespoons onion powder

2 tablespoons oregano

2 tablespoons paprika

1 tablespoon thyme (optional)

FOR THE CHILI

1¼ pounds lean ground turkey

1 large onion, chopped

1 garlic clove, minced

1½ cups frozen corn kernels

1 red bell pepper, chopped

1 green bell pepper, chopped

1 (28-ounce) can no-salt-added crushed tomatoes

1 (15-ounce) can no-salt-added black beans, drained and rinsed

1 (8-ounce) can no-salt-added tomato sauce

Shredded Swiss cheese, finely chopped red onion, unsalted tortilla chips, for topping

TO MAKE THE CHILI SEASONING

1. Add the chili powder, garlic powder, cumin, onion powder, oregano, paprika, and thyme to a glass jar.

2. Shake to mix.

TO MAKE THE CHILI

1. In a large skillet over medium-high heat, add the turkey, onion, and garlic, stirring to crumble the turkey, and cook until no longer pink, 7 to 10 minutes. Drain.

2. Spoon the turkey mixture into a slow cooker, then stir in the corn, bell peppers, tomatoes, black beans, tomato sauce, and 3 tablespoons of the chili seasoning mix.

3. Cook on low for 6 to 8 hours, or high for 4 to 5 hours. Serve topped with desired toppings.

Tip: Store the remaining chili seasoning in a cool, dry, dark area.

PER SERVING Calories: 464; Total Fat 12g; Saturated Fat: 3g; Cholesterol: 100mg; Sodium: 202mg; Potassium: 956mg; Total Carbohydrate: 56g; Fiber: 13g; Protein: 40g

Mixed Baby Greens with Peaches, Fennel, and Walnuts

Serves 4 / Prep time: 10 minutes

Nutritious salads can be prepared with little effort by using prewashed mixed salad greens available at most supermarkets. Topped with peaches, fennel, and walnuts, a serving of this recipe provides heart-healthy omega-3 fats, protein, vitamins, minerals, and fiber to keep you feeling full.

6 cups mixed salad greens

1 medium fennel bulb, trimmed and thinly sliced

2 medium peaches, pits removed, quartered and thinly sliced

2 tablespoons grated Parmesan cheese

¼ cup toasted walnuts, coarsely chopped

1½ tablespoons extra-virgin olive oil

4 tablespoons balsamic vinegar

Freshly ground black pepper

1. Divide the salad greens among 4 plates. Scatter the fennel and peach slices over the greens.

2. Sprinkle each serving with Parmesan cheese and walnuts.

3. Drizzle the olive oil and vinegar over the salads, and season with black pepper. Serve immediately.

Tip: Resembling a rounded, swollen cluster of celery stalks with green-tinged ribs, fennel has a mild, sweet licorice flavor. Strip away the outer, coarse layer of the fennel bulb before slicing or chopping for recipes.

Storage: This salad is best eaten immediately. You could also prepare the salad greens up through step 2 and store in the refrigerator for up to 1 day, and finish just before serving.

PER SERVING Calories: 168; Total Fat 11g; Saturated Fat: 2g; Cholesterol: 2mg; Sodium: 138mg; Potassium: 374mg; Total Carbohydrate: 15g; Fiber: 5g; Protein: 5g

English Cucumber Salad

Serves 4 / Prep time: 5 minutes / Cook time: 5 minutes

SODIUM

LOWEST

MEATLESS
DAIRY-FREE
GLUTEN-FREE
LOW-FAT

English cucumbers, also known as seedless or burpless, are typically longer than regular cucumbers and have a milder flavor. The skin is thinner and it contains smaller, less noticeable seeds, giving them an almost sweet taste that is perfect for a refreshing salad.

FOR THE DRESSING

2 tablespoons balsamic vinegar

1 ½ tablespoons extra-virgin olive oil

1 tablespoon finely chopped
  fresh rosemary

1 tablespoon no-salt stone-
  ground mustard

FOR THE SALAD

1 (8 to 9 inches long) unpeeled
  English cucumber, washed and
  thinly sliced

½ cup grape tomatoes, halved

½ red onion, thinly sliced

Freshly ground black pepper

TO MAKE THE DRESSING

1. In a small saucepan over low heat, heat the vinegar, olive oil, and rosemary. Gently cook for 5 minutes to blend and intensify the flavors.

2. Remove from heat and whisk in the mustard until well blended.

TO MAKE THE SALAD

In a serving bowl, add the cucumber, tomatoes, and red onion. Pour the dressing over the vegetables and toss to coat evenly. Season with black pepper. Serve immediately.

Storage: You can refrigerate this salad for up to 1 day in an airtight container before serving.

PER SERVING Calories: 77; Total Fat 5g; Saturated Fat: 1g; Cholesterol: 0mg; Sodium: 3mg; Potassium: 3mg; Total Carbohydrate: 7g; Fiber: 1g; Protein: 1g

Thai Chicken Broccoli Soup

Serves 4 / Prep time: 10 minutes / Cook time: 20 minutes

This sweet and spicy soup is a Thai takeout staple, a cuisine with dishes that are traditionally known for attention to balanced flavors (sour, sweet, salty, bitter, and spicy). You can create your own healthy version at home for a fraction of the sodium—and cost—with this easy and delicious recipe.

12 ounces boneless, skinless
  chicken breast, fat removed
1½ cups low sodium chicken broth
1 cup canned coconut milk
1 cup white mushrooms, quartered
2 cups broccoli florets
5 slices fresh ginger, peeled
1 to 2 red chili peppers,
  sliced (optional)

1 stalk lemongrass, cut in half
  and smashed
4 green onions, sliced, white and
  green parts separated
1 teaspoon Thai chili paste
¼ cup roughly chopped
  fresh cilantro
¼ cup roughly chopped fresh basil
Pinch white pepper
1 lemon, sliced

1. Place the chicken breasts in a small saucepan. Cover completely with cold water and place over medium heat. Bring the water to 180°F—just before the water starts to bubble. Poach the chicken for 15 minutes or until cooked to 165°F.

2. While the chicken is poaching, in a medium saucepan over medium heat, add the chicken broth, coconut milk, mushrooms, broccoli, ginger, chili peppers (if using), lemongrass, and whites of the green onions, and bring to a simmer.

3. Add the chili paste and simmer for 10 minutes.

4. Cool the chicken slightly and cut into 1-inch cubes. Add the cubed chicken to the soup.

5. Remove the lemongrass, ginger slices, and chili peppers (if using) with a slotted spoon and discard.

6. Add the cilantro, basil, and white pepper. Serve and garnish with lemon slices and green onions.

Storage: Store leftover soup in an airtight container in the refrigerator for 3 to 4 days.

PER SERVING Calories: 250; Total Fat 14g; Saturated Fat: 10g; Cholesterol: 49mg; Sodium: 100mg; Potassium: 261mg; Total Carbohydrate: 11g; Fiber: 4g; Protein: 23g

Chickpea Burgers with Tahini Sauce p.130

8

MEATLESS ENTRÉES

Slow-Cooker Quinoa–Black Bean Stuffed Peppers

Serves 6 / Prep time: 15 minutes / Cook time: 3 hours on high, 6 hours on low

In this delicious recipe, vitamin C-rich peppers are stuffed with high-fiber and protein-rich quinoa and beans, pepper Jack cheese, enchilada sauce, and spices to create perfectly portioned lunches or dinners for the week. Serve them with freshly chopped cilantro and avocado or your favorite toppings.

6 bell peppers

4 garlic cloves, minced

1 cup uncooked quinoa

1 (14-ounce) can black beans, drained and rinsed

1 (14-ounce) can pinto beans, drained and rinsed

1 cup diced tomatoes

1 cup red enchilada sauce

1 teaspoon chili powder

1 teaspoon cumin

1 teaspoon onion powder

1 cup shredded reduced-fat pepper Jack cheese, divided

1. Cut the tops off the bell peppers and scrape out the ribs and seeds.

2. In a large bowl, combine the garlic, quinoa, beans, tomatoes, enchilada sauce, chili powder, cumin, onion powder, and ⅔ cup of pepper Jack cheese. Fill each pepper with the quinoa mixture.

3. Pour ½ cup water into the bottom of a slow cooker. Sit the peppers in the water bath in the slow cooker. Cover and cook on low for 6 hours, or high for 3 hours.

4. Remove the lid, distribute the remaining cheese over the tops of the peppers, and cover again for a few minutes to melt the cheese. Serve immediately.

Tip: You can reduce the sodium further by using replacing half of the cheese with pureed butternut squash.

Storage: You can store leftover filling in the refrigerator in an airtight container for 1 to 2 days. Cooked and filled peppers can be stored in the refrigerator in an airtight container for 3 to 5 days. Freezing is not recommended.

PER SERVING Calories: 369; Total Fat 7g; Saturated Fat: 0g; Cholesterol: 0mg; Sodium: 331mg; Potassium: 473mg; Total Carbohydrate: 59g; Fiber: 10g; Protein: 20g

Slow-Cooker Wild Rice with White Beans, Walnuts, and Cherries

Serves 8 / Prep time: 20 minutes / Cook time: 5 to 6 hours on low

Wild rice contains a type of fiber shown to reduce cholesterol, while the omega-3 fatty acids in walnuts can lower inflammation in the body. Cherries contain powerful antioxidants and phytochemicals that can lower the risk for heart disease by helping regulate blood pressure. Adding these ingredients into one dish makes this a delicious and nutritious recipe, and using a slow cooker makes preparation a breeze.

3 (14-ounce) cans no-salt vegetable broth

2 (15-ounce) cans great northern beans (or other white bean)

2½ cups wild rice, rinsed and drained

1 cup coarsely shredded carrot

1 cup sliced mushrooms

1 tablespoon butter or margarine, melted

2 teaspoons dried marjoram, crushed

¼ teaspoon freshly ground black pepper

¾ cup chopped green onion

½ cup dried tart cherries

½ cup coarsely chopped walnuts

1. Add the broth, beans, wild rice, carrot, mushrooms, butter, marjoram, and black pepper to a slow cooker.

2. Cover and cook on low for 5 to 6 hours.

3. Turn off the slow cooker. Stir in the green onion, cherries, and walnuts. Cover and let stand for 10 minutes. Serve using a slotted spoon to minimize liquids.

Tip: You can omit the cherries or replace them with another dried fruit and vary the type of nut. For a heartier dish, add additional carrots or another favorite vegetable.

Storage: Cooked wild rice will keep in the refrigerator stored in an airtight container for 4 to 6 days. This dish can also be frozen in heavy-duty freezer bags for up to 6 months.

PER SERVING Calories: 420; Total Fat 7g; Saturated Fat: 1g; Cholesterol: 0mg; Sodium: 109mg; Potassium: 346mg; Total Carbohydrate: 73g; Fiber: 9g; Protein: 17g

Slow-Cooker "Meaty" Vegetarian Chili

Serves 8 / Prep time: 20 minutes / Cook time: 6 to 8 hours on low

This easy and tasty slow-cooker vegetarian recipe is full of plant-based protein from fiber-rich beans and tofu, which gives it a "meaty" feel. Certain to be a family favorite, serve this chili with a fresh garden salad topped with fresh tomatoes and sliced avocado.

2 tablespoons extra-virgin olive oil

4 medium onions, chopped

2 green bell peppers, chopped

2 red bell peppers, chopped

4 garlic cloves, minced

1 (14-ounce) package firm tofu, drained and cubed

4 (15-ounce) cans black beans, drained and rinsed

2 (15-ounce) cans no-salt crushed tomatoes

4 tablespoons chili powder

2 tablespoons dried oregano

2 teaspoons ground cumin

½ teaspoon freshly ground black pepper

2 tablespoons white distilled vinegar

1. Heat the olive oil in a large skillet over medium heat. Add the onions and cook, stirring occasionally, until they begin to soften, about 5 minutes.

2. Add the bell peppers, garlic, and tofu, and cook, stirring until the vegetables are lightly browned and tender, about 5 minutes.

3. Add the black beans to the slow cooker set to low. Stir in the cooked bell pepper mixture and tomatoes.

4. Season with the chili powder, oregano, cumin, black pepper, and vinegar. Stir gently and cover.

5. Cook on low for 6 to 8 hours. Serve immediately.

Tip: If you like a heartier chili, add 2 cups of cubed sweet potato when you add the beans to the slow cooker.

Storage: You can store leftover chili in the refrigerator in airtight covered containers for 3 to 4 days. Chili can also be frozen in airtight containers or heavy-duty freezer bags for 4 to 6 months. Freezing tofu will alter the texture slightly, giving it a meatier texture.

PER SERVING Calories: 337; Total Fat 6g; Saturated Fat: 1g; Cholesterol: 0mg; Sodium: 59mg; Potassium: 714mg; Total Carbohydrate: 55g; Fiber: 14g; Protein: 19g

Slow-Cooker Indian Dal

Serves 6 / Prep time: 20 minutes / Cook time: 6 to 8 hours on low

Dal is a thick stew of red lentils, onions, tomatoes, aromatic herbs, and spices, and is traditional to the Indian subcontinent. High in fiber and protein, this flavorful dish can be eaten on its own or served over hot basmati rice, a baked sweet potato, or with warm chapati bread.

3 cups dry red lentils

8 cups water

1 tablespoon extra-virgin olive oil

2 cups chopped onions

2 cups chopped tomatoes, with their juices

4 garlic cloves, minced

2 tablespoons grated fresh ginger

2 teaspoons coriander

2 teaspoons cumin

2 teaspoons turmeric

1 teaspoon cardamom

⅓ cup chopped fresh cilantro

1. Add the lentils and water to a slow cooker and turn it to low.

2. Meanwhile, heat the olive oil in a medium skillet over medium-high heat. Add the onions, tomatoes, garlic, ginger, coriander, cumin, turmeric, and cardamom and cook until reduced, about 7 minutes.

3. Add the vegetable mixture to the slow cooker, cover and cook on low for 6 to 8 hours.

4. Serve and garnish with the cilantro.

Tip: For a creamier dal, stir in ½ cup of low-fat milk, light coconut milk, or plant-based milk just before serving.

Storage: The dal can be stored in the refrigerator in an airtight container for 3 to 5 days. It can also be frozen in airtight containers or heavy-duty freezer bags for 4 to 6 months.

PER SERVING Calories: 201; Total Fat 3g; Saturated Fat: 0g; Cholesterol: 0mg; Sodium: 18mg; Potassium: 245mg; Total Carbohydrate: 47g; Fiber: 20g; Protein: 14g

Slow-Cooker Chickpea Vegetable Stew

SODIUM

LOWER

MEATLESS
DAIRY-FREE
GLUTEN-FREE
LOW-FAT
ONE-POT

Serves 6 / Prep time: 15 minutes
Cook time: 4 hours on low, 3 hours on high, plus 1 hour on low

Full of fresh vegetables and beans, this hearty stew uses a combination of root vegetables, summer squash, and fresh tomatoes. Seasoned with cumin, onion, and garlic, it makes a filling weekday lunch or a hearty dinner served over cooked quinoa, rice, or barley.

4 large carrots, diagonally sliced into
    2-inch pieces (about 5 cups)
2 medium turnips, peeled and cut
    into 1-inch cubes (about 3 cups)
2 medium parsnips, peeled and cut
    into 1-inch cubes (about 3 cups)
1 large onion, diced (about 1 cup)
3 garlic cloves, minced
2 cups chopped fresh tomatoes,
    and their juices

2 cups low-sodium vegetable broth
1 teaspoon ground cumin
¼ teaspoon crushed red
    pepper flakes
2 medium zucchini, cut into
    ½-inch-thick slices
2 (15-ounce) cans chickpeas,
    drained and rinsed

1. Combine the carrots, turnips, parsnips, onion, garlic, tomatoes and their juices, broth, cumin, and red pepper flakes in a slow cooker.

2. Cover and cook on low heat for 6 hours, or on high for 3 hours.

3. Turn the heat setting to low and add the zucchini and chickpeas. Cook for 1 hour more and serve.

Tip: This stew can be served over cooked grains or a baked sweet potato.

Storage: You can store leftover stew in the refrigerator in airtight covered containers for 3 to 4 days. The stew can also be frozen in airtight containers or heavy-duty freezer bags for 4 to 6 months.

PER SERVING Calories: 248; Total Fat 1g; Saturated Fat: 0g; Cholesterol: 0mg; Sodium: 134mg; Potassium: 762mg; Total Carbohydrate: 51g; Fiber: 13g; Protein: 11g

Slow-Cooker Squash Lasagna

Serves 6 / Prep time: 15 minutes / Cook time: 3 to 4 hours on low

Creamy butternut squash replaces traditional tomato sauce in this lower sodium squash lasagna recipe. Full of protein, vitamins, minerals, and fiber, whole wheat noodles are layered between winter squash, baby spinach, creamy ricotta, and mozzarella. With just 15 minutes of prep time, you can turn your slow cooker on, walk away, and come back to a nutritious dinner in a few hours.

2 (12-ounce) packages frozen winter squash puree, thawed

⅛ teaspoon ground nutmeg

1 (24-ounce) container light ricotta cheese (about 3 cups)

1 (5-ounce) package baby spinach (6 cups)

¼ teaspoon freshly ground black pepper

12 whole wheat lasagna noodles

8 ounces grated part-skim mozzarella cheese (about 2 cups)

1.   In a medium bowl, mix the squash and nutmeg.

2.   In a second bowl, combine the ricotta, spinach, and black pepper.

3. In the bottom of a slow cooker, spread one-fourth of the squash mixture. Top with 3 lasagna noodles (breaking to fit if necessary), one-third of the remaining squash mixture, 3 lasagna noodles, and half the ricotta mixture. Repeat layering, using half of the remaining squash, 3 lasagna noodles, the remaining squash, the remaining 3 lasagna noodles, and ending with the remaining ricotta mixture. Sprinkle with the mozzarella.

4. Cover and cook on low until the noodles are tender, 3 to 4 hours.

Tip: You can boost the vegetable content of this recipe by adding 2 cups of frozen broccoli to the ricotta and spinach mixture.

Storage: You can store cooked lasagna in an airtight container in the refrigerator for 3 to 5 days. You can freeze lasagna in covered airtight containers or heavy-duty freezer bags, or wrap tightly with heavy-duty aluminum foil for 1 to 2 months.

PER SERVING Calories: 462; Total Fat 13g; Saturated Fat: 7g; Cholesterol: 50mg; Sodium: 372mg; Potassium: 1mg; Total Carbohydrate: 61g; Fiber: 9g; Protein: 28g

Slow-Cooker Red Beans and Rice

Serves 8 / Prep time: 10 minutes
Cook time: 6 to 8 hours on low, plus overnight to soak the bean

Easy to make, meat-free, and full of filling protein and fiber, this Creole-inspired red beans and rice recipe makes a hearty and delicious meal, complete with the "trinity" of onions, bell peppers, and celery. Liquid smoke and chipotle peppers add a smoky-spicy vibrant flavor.

1 pound dry red kidney beans,
  soaked overnight
5 garlic cloves, minced
1 large onion, finely diced
  (about 1½ cups)
5 celery stalks, finely diced
  (about 1½ cups)
1 large green bell pepper, finely
  diced (about 1½ cups)
3 bay leaves
2 teaspoons dried thyme
2 teaspoons dried oregano

½ teaspoon red pepper flakes
½ teaspoon freshly ground
  black pepper
2 chipotle peppers in adobo
  sauce, chopped
½ tablespoon red pepper sauce
1 teaspoon liquid smoke
7 cups water
Cooked white or brown rice,
  for serving
Chopped green onion, for garnish

1. Drain the soaked beans, rinse under water, and place in a slow cooker.

2. Add the garlic, onion, celery, bell pepper, bay leaves, thyme, oregano, red pepper flakes, black pepper, chipotle peppers, red pepper sauce, and liquid smoke to the slow cooker. Pour the water on top and stir to combine.

3. Cook on high for 6 to 8 hours or until the beans are soft and cooked through. Remove and discard the bay leaf.

4. Serve immediately over rice, garnished with green onion.

Storage: You can store leftover red beans in the refrigerator in airtight, covered containers for 3 to 4 days. Red beans can also be frozen in airtight containers or heavy-duty freezer bags for 4 to 6 months.

PER SERVING Calories: 292; Total Fat 7g; Saturated Fat: 1g; Cholesterol: 0mg; Sodium: 172mg; Potassium: 218mg; Total Carbohydrate: 41g; Fiber: 10g; Protein: 14g

Broccoli, Peas, and Whole Grain Rigatoni

SODIUM

LOWER

MEATLESS

Serves 2 / Prep time: 5 minutes / Cook time: 20 minutes

Broccoli is rich in the antioxidant vitamins A and C, as well as the phyto-chemicals, indoles, and flavonoids important for reducing inflammation in the body. Used in this high fiber and quick and easy recipe, broccoli and peas are steamed and tossed with fiber-rich, whole grain rigatoni.

4 ounces whole grain
 rigatoni noodles
2 cups broccoli florets
1 cup frozen green peas, thawed
2 tablespoons Parmesan cheese

2 teaspoons extra-virgin olive oil
2 teaspoons minced garlic
Freshly ground black pepper
¼ cup chopped fresh basil

1. Fill a large pot of water and bring it to a boil. Add the pasta and cook until al dente, according to the package directions. Drain the pasta.

2. While the pasta is cooking, in a pot fitted with a steamer basket, bring 1 inch of water to a boil. Add the broccoli and peas, cover and steam until tender, about 10 minutes.

3. In a large bowl, combine the cooked pasta and broccoli. Toss with the Parmesan cheese, olive oil, and garlic. Season with black pepper.

4. Serve immediately and garnish with fresh basil.

Tip: To boost the protein content of this dish, choose a protein-fortified whole grain pasta.

Storage: This dish can be stored in the refrigerator in airtight containers for 3 to 5 days. It can also be frozen in airtight containers or heavy-duty freezer bags for 1 to 2 months.

PER SERVING Calories: 358; Total Fat 8g; Saturated Fat: 2g; Cholesterol: 4mg; Sodium: 198mg; Potassium: 434mg; Total Carbohydrate: 57g; Fiber: 11g; Protein: 16g

Southwestern Veggie Bowl

Serves 6 / Prep time: 10 minutes / Cook time: 55 to 60 minutes

This one-bowl vegan meal is loaded with vitamins A, C, and K, and is high in cholesterol-lowering fiber. Seasoned with fresh herbs and spices, this very low-sodium meal is full of colorful and nutrient-dense veggies and protein-rich beans.

2 teaspoons extra-virgin olive oil

2 cups chopped green bell pepper

1 cup chopped red onion

4 garlic cloves, minced

1 chili pepper, minced

1 cup diced sweet potato

1 cup chopped tomato

1 cup brown rice

1 cup green lentils

1 tablespoon ground cumin

½ tablespoon freshly ground
    black pepper

1 tablespoon red wine vinegar

2 cups no-salt-added
    vegetable stock

2 cups water

4 cups chopped kale leaves

1 cup cooked black beans

2 tablespoons minced fresh cilantro

4 lime wedges, for garnish

1. In a large sauté pan, heat the olive oil over medium-high heat. Add the bell pepper, onion, garlic, chili pepper, sweet potato, and tomato and cook until the onions begin to look translucent, 10 to 15 minutes.

2. Add the rice, lentils, cumin, black pepper, vinegar, stock, and water. Bring to a boil and reduce the heat to a simmer. Cover and cook for 45 minutes.

3. Add the kale, black beans and cilantro. Stir to mix. Garnish with lime wedges and serve.

Tip: You can reduce the cooking time in step 2 to 30 minutes by precooking the sweet potato in the microwave on high for 3 minutes.

Storage: You can store leftover cooked rice and beans in the refrigerator in airtight covered containers for 3 to 4 days. The rice and beans (without the kale) can also be frozen in airtight containers or heavy-duty freezer bags for 4 to 6 months.

PER SERVING Calories: 330; Total Fat 4g; Saturated Fat: 0g; Cholesterol: 0mg; Sodium: 70mg; Potassium: 624mg; Total Carbohydrate: 64g; Fiber: 13g; Protein: 15g

Cauliflower Fried Rice

Serves 2 / Prep time: 10 minutes / Cook time: 15 to 21 minutes

There's no need to give up your favorite Chinese food when following a sodium-restricted diet. Instead, prepare this nutritious low-sodium version of fried rice using nothing but veggies, with low-sodium broth and fresh spices replacing high-sodium soy sauce. Low in calories, this dish is certain to satisfy that craving for take-out.

2 cups cauliflower florets (one head)

1 tablespoon sesame oil, divided

1 red onion, sliced

4 garlic cloves, minced

1 tablespoon minced fresh ginger

1 small red chile, thinly sliced

1 cup frozen green peas, thawed

2 cups broccoli florets

1 large carrot, julienned

½ red bell pepper, diced

2 eggs, beaten

¼ cup low-sodium vegetable broth

2 tablespoons pumpkin seeds

2 tablespoons fresh cilantro leaves

1. Pulse the cauliflower florets in a food processor until finely chopped.

2. Heat ½ tablespoon of the sesame oil in a large skillet over medium heat. Add the onion, garlic, ginger, and chile and cook, stirring, until the onion is tender, about 5 minutes.

3. Add the remaining ½ tablespoon oil, the cauliflower, peas, broccoli, carrot, and bell pepper and continue to cook, stirring frequently, for 2 to 3 minutes.

4. Add the vegetable broth and steam, covered, until the broth has evaporated and vegetables are tender, about 6 minutes.

5. Move the vegetables to one side, add the beaten eggs, and stir quickly and thoroughly to scramble, and then mix to combine the eggs with the vegetables. Continue to cook for 2 to 3 minutes.

6. Remove from heat and serve topped with pumpkin seeds and fresh cilantro.

Tip: You can cut down on preparation time by buying riced cauliflower, available in the produce section of major supermarkets.

Storage: Leftover cauliflower fried rice can be stored in the refrigerator in an airtight container for 4 to 5 days. Freezing this dish is not recommended, as it will alter the texture of the vegetables.

PER SERVING Calories: 328; Total Fat 14g; Saturated Fat: 3g; Cholesterol: 186mg; Sodium: 272mg; Potassium: 1215mg; Total Carbohydrate: 39g; Fiber: 12g; Protein: 18g

Polenta with Fresh Vegetables

Serves 4 / Prep time: 10 minutes / Cook time: 40 minutes

Polenta is a traditional Italian ingredient made from fine or coarsely ground cornmeal. Considered a whole grain, polenta is packed with nutrients important for heart health, including vitamins A and C, and the carotenoids lutein and zeaxanthin. Topped with lightly steamed vegetables, this creamy low-sodium dish has added flavor from Parmesan cheese.

Cooking spray

1 cup polenta

4 cups water

1 teaspoon chopped garlic

1 cup sliced mushrooms

1 cup sliced red onion

1 cup broccoli florets

1 cup sliced fresh green beans

1 cup sliced yellow squash

2 tablespoons grated
    Parmesan cheese

Chopped fresh basil

1. Heat the oven to 350°F. Lightly coat a 3-quart ovenproof dish with cooking spray.

2. Combine the polenta, water, and garlic in the prepared dish. Bake uncovered until the polenta pulls away from the sides of the baking dish, about 40 minutes. The polenta should be moist.

3. While the polenta is cooking, spray a nonstick frying pan with cooking spray. Add the mushrooms and onion and sauté over medium heat until the vegetables are tender, about 5 minutes.

4. In a pot fitted with a steamer basket, bring 1 inch of water to a boil. Add the broccoli, green beans, and squash. Cover and steam until the vegetables are tender-crisp, 2 to 3 minutes.

5. When the polenta is done, top with the cooked vegetables. Sprinkle with Parmesan cheese and fresh basil. Serve immediately.

Tip: Try any combination of vegetables, including leafy greens.

Storage: For best results, serve polenta right away, as it is meant to be creamy. While you can refrigerate polenta in an airtight container for 5 to 7 days, the polenta will become firm, in which case you may consider slicing it and lightly frying it. It is not recommended to freeze polenta.

PER SERVING Calories: 179; Total Fat 2g; Saturated Fat: 1g; Cholesterol: 3mg; Sodium: 53mg; Potassium: 336mg; Total Carbohydrate: 35g; Fiber: 5g; Protein: 7g

Creole-Style Black-Eyed Peas with Spinach

Serves 4 / Prep time: 10 minutes / Cook time: 10 minutes

Black-eyed peas are an important source of folate, a B vitamin needed for a healthy heart. This simple and quick skillet dish is inspired by Southern-style black-eyed peas. For a speedy supper, serve this dish with sliced tomatoes or over cooked brown rice or polenta.

1 tablespoon extra-virgin olive oil

1 medium onion, chopped

1 medium green bell pepper, chopped

4 garlic cloves, chopped

10 ounces fresh spinach, rinsed, stemmed, and coarsely chopped

1 cup chopped tomatoes, and their juices

2 (15-ounce) cans black-eyed peas, drained and rinsed

Freshly ground black pepper

Pinch crushed red pepper flakes (optional)

1. In a large skillet over medium-high heat, heat the olive oil. Add the onion, bell pepper, and garlic and sauté until the onion is translucent, about 5 minutes.

2. Add the spinach and tomatoes and cook, stirring, until spinach is wilted, 2 to 3 minutes.

3. Add the black-eyed peas, black pepper, and red pepper flakes (if using). Bring to a simmer over medium heat and heat through, 3 to 5 minutes. Serve immediately.

Tip: This recipe calls for canned beans, but fresh are best if you can get them. You could also use frozen or prepare dried beans; once they are cooked, the recipe is the same.

Storage: You can store leftover black-eyed peas in the refrigerator in airtight containers for 3 to 4 days. Leftover portions can also be frozen in airtight containers or heavy-duty freezer bags for 4 to 6 months.

PER SERVING Calories: 276; Total Fat 4g; Saturated Fat: 1g; Cholesterol: 0mg; Sodium: 62mg; Potassium: 650mg; Total Carbohydrate: 46g; Fiber: 12g; Protein: 16g

Black Bean Croquettes with Fresh Salsa

Serves 4 / Prep time: 10 minutes / Cook time: 20 minutes

This creative and nutritious recipe transforms a handful of staple pantry ingredients into a high-protein vegetarian meal in minutes. Canned black beans and frozen corn are made into spicy croquettes for a dinner that can be ready in under 30 minutes.

Cooking spray

2 (15-ounce) cans black beans, drained and rinsed

4 garlic cloves, minced

1 teaspoon ground cumin

1 cup frozen corn kernels

¼ cup plain dry breadcrumbs, plus ⅓ cup

2 cups finely chopped tomatoes

4 green onions, sliced

½ cup chopped fresh cilantro

1 teaspoon chili powder, divided

Pinch paprika

1 tablespoon extra-virgin olive oil

1 avocado, sliced

1. Preheat the oven to 425°F. Coat a baking sheet with cooking spray.

2. Mash the black beans, garlic, and cumin with a fork in a large bowl until no whole beans remain. Stir in corn and ¼ cup of the breadcrumbs.

3. Combine tomatoes, green onions, cilantro, ½ teaspoon of the chili powder, and paprika in a medium bowl. Stir 1 cup of the tomato salsa mixture into the black bean mixture.

4. Mix the remaining ⅓ cup breadcrumbs, the olive oil, and the remaining ½ teaspoon chili powder in a small bowl until the breadcrumbs are coated with oil. Divide the bean mixture into 8 scant ½-cup balls. Lightly press each bean ball into the breadcrumb mixture, turning to coat. Place on the prepared baking sheet.

5. Bake the croquettes until heated through and the breadcrumbs are golden brown, about 20 minutes. Stir the avocado into the remaining tomato mixture. Serve the remaining salsa with the croquettes.

Tip: For added nutrition and fiber, add 1 cup riced cauliflower to the bean mash.

Storage: Cooked croquettes can be stored in the refrigerator, wrapped individually in an airtight container for 5 to 7 days. You can also freeze them by wrapping them individually and storing in an airtight container for 1 to 2 months.

PER SERVING Calories: 426; Total Fat 12g; Saturated Fat: 2g; Cholesterol: 0mg; Sodium: 135mg; Potassium: 595mg; Total Carbohydrate: 66g; Fiber: 16g; Protein: 18g

Sweet Potato Egg Cups

Serves 2 / Prep time: 2 minutes / Cook time: 26 minutes

This uncomplicated and wonderfully filling recipe uses just two main ingredients: sweet potatoes and eggs. Sweet potatoes are high in fiber and the important antioxidant beta-carotene, and eggs have high-quality protein. The recipe is easily doubled, tripled, and even quadrupled, and you can vary the seasonings according to your taste preferences.

2 very large sweet potatoes

Cooking spray

1 teaspoon extra-virgin olive oil

4 eggs

Freshly ground black pepper

Sriracha, or other hot sauce

Freshly chopped parsley, or cilantro, for garnish

1. Preheat the oven to 350°F.

2. Scrub the sweet potatoes, prick all over with a fork, place on a glass baking dish, and cover with a damp paper towel. Microwave on high for 3 minutes. Turn the baking dish and microwave until potatoes are tender when pricked with a fork, about 3 minutes more. Let them cool slightly.

3. Remove potatoes from the baking dish and mist the dish with cooking spray. Slice each potato in half lengthwise. Using a paring knife, carefully carve out a well in the center of each half big enough for the size of your eggs. Crack one egg at a time into a small bowl and then pour into the well. Place the potato halves back into the baking dish, resting them against the side of the pan if needed to keep them from tipping and spilling any egg.

4. Season with black pepper and mist with cooking spray. Bake for 20 minutes, or until the eggs are cooked to your liking.

5. Remove from the oven and serve topped with your favorite hot sauce and fresh herbs.

Tip: This recipe could easily be made using russet potatoes in place of the sweet potatoes.

Storage: Refrigerate the cooked potatoes and egg in an airtight container for 3 to 4 days. Freezing is not recommended.

PER SERVING Calories: 369; Total Fat 12g; Saturated Fat: 4g; Cholesterol: 372mg; Sodium: 167mg; Potassium: 536mg; Total Carbohydrate: 48g; Fiber: 6g; Protein: 16g

Greek Omelet

SODIUM

LOW

MEATLESS
GLUTEN-FREE

Serves 2 / Prep time: 10 minutes / Cook time: 5 to 7 minutes

This ultra-quick and nutritious omelet has flavors reminiscent of Greece and yields the perfect amount for a light dinner when served with a fresh green salad. To cut down on prep time, I use frozen spinach, although feel free to substitute with fresh instead.

½ cup frozen spinach, thawed

4 large eggs

¼ cup crumbled feta cheese

4 green onions, thinly sliced

3 tablespoons chopped
   fresh parsley

2 tablespoons chopped fresh dill

1 tablespoon chopped fresh mint

Pinch nutmeg

Freshly ground black pepper

2 teaspoons extra-virgin olive oil

1. Squeeze the spinach to remove excess water.

2. Blend the eggs with a fork in a medium bowl. Add the feta, green onions, parsley, dill, mint, nutmeg, black pepper, and spinach to the eggs and mix gently.

3. Preheat the broiler with an oven rack about 4 inches from the heat source.

4. Add the olive oil to a 10-inch nonstick skillet over medium heat. Pour in the egg mixture and tilt to distribute evenly. Reduce the heat to medium-low and cook until the bottom is light golden, lifting the edges to allow uncooked egg to flow underneath, 3 to 4 minutes.

5. Place the pan under the broiler and cook until the top is set, 1½ to 2½ minutes.

6. Slide the omelet onto a platter and cut into wedges. Serve immediately.

Tip: For an equally nutritious variation, substitute cooked kale in place of the spinach.

Storage: You can store cooked omelet in the refrigerator in an airtight container for 3 to 4 days. Freezing of whole cooked eggs is not recommended, as whites will become tough and rubbery.

PER SERVING Calories: 257; Total Fat 18g; Saturated Fat: 7g; Cholesterol: 389mg; Sodium: 386mg; Potassium: 326mg; Total Carbohydrate: 7g; Fiber: 3g; Protein: 17g

Simple Southwest Tofu Scramble

Serves 4 / Prep time: 10 minutes / Cook time: 15 to 17 minutes

This quick and easy one-pan tofu scramble minimizes the use of salt by using a mix of bold Southwestern spices and flavorful vegetables so you can have a nutritious high-protein, filling dinner on the table in less than 30 minutes. Serve with a salad, toast, potatoes, or fruit, with sides of salsa or avocado slices.

FOR THE SAUCE

1 teaspoon chili powder

1 teaspoon cumin powder

1 teaspoon paprika

½ teaspoon turmeric

¼ cup water

FOR THE SCRAMBLE

16 ounces extra-firm low-sodium tofu

1 tablespoon extra-virgin olive oil

½ red onion, thinly sliced

1 red bell pepper, thinly sliced

4 garlic cloves, minced

1 (15-ounce) can black beans, drained and rinsed

1 cup sliced mushrooms

4 cups kale, loosely chopped

TO MAKE THE SAUCE

In a small bowl, mix the chili powder, cumin, paprika, turmeric, and water. Set aside.

TO MAKE THE SCRAMBLE

1. Pat tofu dry and wrap it in a clean, absorbent towel. Then place a heavy object, such as a skillet, on top of the wrapped tofu. Let it sit for 15 minutes; the towel will absorb moisture.

2. While the tofu is draining, heat the olive oil in a large skillet over medium heat. Add the onion, bell pepper, and garlic and cook until softened, about 5 minutes.

3. Add the black beans, mushrooms, and kale and cover to steam for 2 minutes.

4. Meanwhile, unwrap the tofu and use a fork to crumble it into bite-sized pieces.

5. Move the veggies to one side of the pan and add the tofu. Sauté for 2 minutes, then add the sauce, pouring it mostly over the tofu with some poured over the vegetables.

6. Stir immediately to evenly distribute the sauce. Cook for another 5 to 7 minutes until the tofu is slightly browned.

Storage: You can store cooked tofu in the refrigerator in an airtight container for 3 to 4 days. You can also freeze it in an airtight container or heavy-duty freezer bags for 1 to 2 months, however the texture will change noticeably and it will be a bit more spongy.

PER SERVING Calories: 280; Total Fat 10g; Saturated Fat: 2g; Cholesterol: 0mg; Sodium: 54mg; Potassium: 694mg; Total Carbohydrate: 33g; Fiber: 10g; Protein: 20g

Chickpea Burgers with Tahini Sauce

Serves 4 / Prep time: 10 minutes / Cook time: 10 minutes

These healthy meatless burgers are a lighter version of falafel, which is typically deep-fried. High in fiber and plant-powered protein from chickpeas, these easy and delicious burgers can be made in minutes. A flavorful tahini sauce finishes the burgers, which are topped with sliced red onion and minced cucumbers.

FOR THE TAHINI SAUCE

½ cup plain low-fat Greek yogurt

2 tablespoons tahini

1 tablespoon lemon juice

½ cup chopped flat-leaf parsley

FOR THE BURGERS

1 (19-ounce) can chickpeas, drained and rinsed

1 garlic clove, minced

1 ½ teaspoons ground coriander

1 ½ teaspoons ground cumin

Freshly ground black pepper

1 medium carrot, grated

1 large egg

2 tablespoons all-purpose flour

2 tablespoons extra-virgin olive oil

2 (6-inch) whole wheat pitas, halved

1 cup baby spinach (optional)

1 red onion, sliced

1 Persian cucumber, minced

TO MAKE THE TAHINI SAUCE

In a medium bowl, combine the yogurt, tahini, lemon juice, and parsley. Set aside.

1. Add the chickpeas, garlic, coriander, cumin, and black pepper to a food processor. Process to a rough paste, then add the carrot, egg, and flour. Process briefly until evenly mixed but slightly rough. The mixture will be moist. Form into 4 patties.

2. Heat the olive oil in a large nonstick skillet over medium-high heat. Add the patties and cook until golden and beginning to crisp, 4 to 5 minutes. Carefully flip and cook until golden brown, 2 to 4 minutes more.

3. Warm the pitas if desired. Divide the chickpea patties among the pita halves and add the baby spinach (if using) to the pockets. Serve with the tahini sauce, onion, and cucumber.

Storage: You can store leftover burgers and tahini sauce in airtight containers in the refrigerator for 3 to 5 days. The burgers freeze well; wrap tightly in plastic wrap or foil and store in airtight freezer bags for up to 3 months.

PER SERVING Calories: 351; Total Fat 14g; Saturated Fat: 2g; Cholesterol: 47mg; Sodium: 135mg; Potassium: 198mg; Total Carbohydrate: 45g; Fiber: 9g; Protein: 17g

Eggplant "Parmesan" Marinara

Serves 10 / Prep time: 25 minutes / Cook time: 55 minutes

I came up with the idea for this recipe during my grill-only phase, and eggplant is an excellent vegetable to grill. Pan-fried eggplant tends to be too soft and grainy for my tastes. Grilling the eggplant gives it a nice meaty texture and taste.

2 eggs, beaten

4 cups Panko bread crumbs

3 eggplants, peeled and
thinly sliced

6 cups low sodium spaghetti
sauce, divided (such as
L.E. Roselli brand)

1 (16-ounce) package Swiss cheese,
shredded and divided

½ cup crumbled ricotta, divided

½ teaspoon dried basil

1. Preheat the oven to 350°F.

2. Place the eggs and bread crumbs in two separate wide-bottomed bowls. Dip the eggplant first in the eggs, then in the bread crumbs, and place in a single layer on a baking sheet.

3. Bake for 5 minutes, flip the slices over, and bake for an additional 5 minutes.

4. In a 9x13 inch baking dish spread 3 cups of the spaghetti sauce to cover the bottom.

5. Place a layer of eggplant slices on the sauce. Sprinkle with half the Swiss and ricotta cheeses. Repeat with the remaining ingredients, ending with the cheeses. Sprinkle basil on top.

6. Bake until golden brown, about 35 minutes.

PER SERVING Calories: 391; Total Fat 17g; Saturated Fat: 9g; Cholesterol: 85mg; Sodium: 221mg; Potassium: 434mg; Total Carbohydrate: 42g; Fiber: 7g; Protein: 22g

Lemon Quinoa and Peas

Serves 4 / Prep time: 5 minutes / Cook time: 20 to 27 minutes

SODIUM

LOWEST

MEATLESS
DAIRY-FREE
GLUTEN-FREE
LOW-FAT
ONE-POT

This recipe uses just a few pantry staples yet produces maximum flavor. Protein- and fiber-packed quinoa is easy to cook in one pot and serves as a hearty substitute for meat any day of the week. Green peas add heart-healthy vitamins and plant protein, while pine nuts add healthy fats.

1 cup dry quinoa

1 cup no-salt-added
   vegetable stock

⅓ cup freshly squeezed lemon juice

½ cup water

½ cup pine nuts

1 cup frozen peas

1. In a medium saucepan, mix together the quinoa, stock, lemon juice, and water and bring to a boil. Reduce the heat to low, cover, and cook until liquid has been absorbed, about 15 minutes.

2. While the quinoa is cooking, toast the pine nuts in a small frying pan over high heat, stirring continuously until browned, 3 to 4 minutes.

3. Once quinoa is cooked, add the frozen peas and let sit for 2 to 3 minutes, or until peas are defrosted.

4. Top with pine nuts and serve immediately.

Tip: You can boost the protein further by replacing the peas with frozen shelled edamame and cooking for 5 minutes. Can't find quinoa or not a fan? Substitute with brown rice instead.

Storage: Leftovers can be stored in the refrigerator in an airtight container for 2 to 3 days. You can also freeze the cooked quinoa in an airtight container or heavy-duty freezer bag for 1 to 2 months.

PER SERVING Calories: 309; Total Fat 14g; Saturated Fat: 1g; Cholesterol: 0mg; Sodium: 86mg; Potassium: 170mg; Total Carbohydrate: 38g Fiber: 5g; Protein: 10g

Shrimp Jambalaya p.153

9

FISH AND SEAFOOD ENTRÉES

Slow-Cooker Shrimp and Artichoke Sorghum Risotto

Serve 4 / Prep time: 30 minutes / Cook time: 3 to 4 hours

The gluten-free whole grain sorghum imparts a sweet flavor and high levels of antioxidants, including a compound called policosanol—important for heart health—to this slow cooker shrimp dish. Full of protein, fiber, and several servings of vegetables, the use of a slow-cooker makes it easy to prepare this sophisticated dish.

1 tablespoon extra-virgin olive oil

1 cup chopped yellow onion

4 garlic cloves, minced

1 red bell pepper, chopped

¼ cup freshly squeezed lemon juice

1 cup whole grain sorghum, rinsed

3 cups low-sodium chicken broth

¼ cup chopped sun-dried tomatoes, not packed in oil

1 (12-ounce) package frozen quartered artichoke hearts

½ teaspoon freshly ground black pepper

1 pound large shrimp, peeled and deveined (uncooked, thawed if frozen)

2 ounces Pecorino-Romano cheese, grated

4 ounces baby spinach

⅓ cup chopped fresh parsley

1. Heat the olive oil in a nonstick skillet over medium-low heat. Add the onion and sauté until translucent, about 5 minutes.

2. Add the garlic and bell pepper and cook for 1 more minute.

3. Add the lemon juice, increase the heat to medium, and cook until liquid is absorbed, about 1 minute.

4. Transfer the onion mixture to the slow cooker and stir in the sorghum, broth, sun-dried tomatoes, artichokes, and black pepper.

5. Cover and cook on high 3 to 4 hours, until sorghum is tender and the liquid is almost absorbed.

6. About 15 minutes before serving, stir in the shrimp and cheese. Cover and continue to cook on high for another 10 minutes, or until shrimp are opaque.

7. Fold in the baby spinach, stirring until it is wilted. Stir in parsley and divide among serving bowls. Serve immediately.

Tip: You can easily replace the sorghum with pearl barley, an equally nutritious grain, for a more traditional risotto.

Storage: The cooked risotto can be stored in the refrigerator in an airtight container for 3 to 4 days. It can also be frozen in an airtight container or heavy-duty freezer bags for 4 to 6 months.

PER SERVING Calories: 336; Total Fat 6g; Saturated Fat: 1g; Cholesterol: 138mg; Sodium: 354mg; Potassium: 409mg; Total Carbohydrate: 49g; Fiber: 6g; Protein: 27g

Slow-Cooker Seafood Stew

Serves 6 / Prep time: 10 minutes / Cook time: 4 hours 30 to 45 minutes

This hearty seafood stew is made using a variety of fresh seafood, vegetables, and seasonings, making the finished product rich and savory while keeping the sodium content in check. Each serving provides a balanced meal high in protein, fiber, heart-healthy fats, and essential vitamins and minerals. Serve with crusty whole grain bread.

2 cups chopped onion

2 medium stalks celery, finely chopped

4 ounces frozen spinach

5 garlic cloves, minced

1 (28-ounce) can no-salt-added diced tomatoes, undrained

½ cup low-sodium vegetable broth

1 tablespoon red wine vinegar

1 tablespoon extra-virgin olive oil

3 teaspoons no-salt lemon pepper seasoning

¼ teaspoon sugar

¼ teaspoon crushed red pepper flakes

¼ cup chopped fresh parsley

1 pound cod fillets, cut into 1-inch pieces

¼ pound uncooked medium shrimp, shells and tails removed

¼ pound scallops

¼ pound crab meat

1. Add the onion, celery, spinach, garlic, tomatoes, broth, vinegar, olive oil, lemon pepper seasoning, sugar, red pepper flakes, and parsley to a slow cooker. Cover and cook on high for 4 hours.

2. Add the cod, shrimp, scallops, and crab. Cover and cook for an additional 30 to 45 minutes or until the fish is opaque and flakes with a fork.

Tip: You can vary the fish and seafood to fit whatever you have on hand. You could also add ½ pound of baby potatoes cut into small pieces for a heartier stew.

Storage: The seafood stew can be stored in the refrigerator in airtight containers for 3 to 4 days. It can also be frozen in airtight containers or heavy-duty freezer bags for 2 to 3 months.

PER SERVING Calories: 242; Total Fat 4g; Saturated Fat: 0g; Cholesterol: 104mg; Sodium: 331mg; Potassium: 315mg; Total Carbohydrate: 15g; Fiber: 4g; Protein: 36g

Slow-Cooker Lemon Pepper Tilapia with Asparagus and Peppers

Serves 4 / Prep time: 15 minutes
Cook time: 2 to 3 hours on high, depending whether the fish is thawed or frozen

This light dinner uses a slow cooker to steam heart-healthy tilapia with fiber-rich veggies. Tilapia is rich in omega-3 fatty acids, important for reducing inflammation. It is also an excellent source of B vitamins, critical for heart health. The dish goes well with a green salad and cooked brown rice.

4 (6- to 8-ounce) tilapia fillets

4 teaspoons lemon pepper, divided

½ cup freshly squeezed lemon
   juice, divided

4 teaspoons butter, divided

1 pound asparagus, trimmed

1 red bell pepper, sliced

1. Cut 4 large pieces of foil, big enough to make fillet packets.

2. Lay each fillet on a piece of foil and evenly sprinkle each with 1 teaspoon lemon pepper and 2 tablespoons lemon juice. Top each with 1 teaspoon butter.

3. Top each packet with one-quarter of the asparagus and one-quarter of the bell pepper.

4. Fold the foil over the fish, then fold the ends together to seal each packet. Transfer the packets to the slow cooker and cook on high for 2 hours if the fish is thawed, or 3 hours if the fish is frozen. Serve immediately.

Storage: Cooked tilapia can be stored in the refrigerator in an airtight container for 3 to 4 days. It can be frozen in an airtight container or heavy-duty freezer bag for 2 to 3 months.

PER SERVING Calories: 177; Total Fat 6g; Saturated Fat: 3g; Cholesterol: 34mg; Sodium: 29mg; Potassium: 449mg; Total Carbohydrate: 8g; Fiber: 3g; Protein: 26g

Grilled Mahi-Mahi with Pineapple–Red Onion Salsa

Serves 4 / Prep time: 10 minutes / Cook time: 8 minutes

Mahi-mahi is perfect for those who do not like their fish to taste too "fishy." Similar to tilapia, swordfish, and marlin, mahi-mahi is a light fish that really takes to the added flavors of a recipe.

½ cup medium diced fresh pineapple, grilled or un-grilled

¼ cup thinly sliced red onion

½ jalapeño, minced

1½ teaspoons coarsely chopped fresh cilantro

1½ teaspoons coarsely chopped fresh mint

1 tablespoon rice wine vinegar

1 tablespoon freshly squeezed lime juice

2 tablespoons extra-virgin olive oil, plus 1 teaspoon

4 (6-ounce) mahi-mahi fillets

Freshly ground black pepper

1. Preheat a grill.

2. To make the relish, in a bowl mix together the pineapple, red onion, jalapeño, cilantro, mint, vinegar, lime juice, and 1 teaspoon of the olive oil.

3. Coat the mahi-mahi fillets on both sides with the remaining 2 tablespoons olive oil and season with black pepper.

4. Grill over medium high heat until the lightly browned, about 4 minutes per side.

Tip: You can make the relish one day in advance and keep it stored in a covered bowl in the refrigerator.

PER SERVING Calories: 264; Total Fat 10g; Saturated Fat: 1g; Cholesterol: 160mg; Sodium: 191mg; Potassium: 41mg; Total Carbohydrate: 3g; Fiber: 0g; Protein: 40g

Cod with Tomato-Thyme Salsa

Serves 4 / Prep time: 5 minutes / Cook time: 10 to 15 minutes

Cod is a particularly lean fish that is a good source of inflammation-reducing heart-healthy omega-3 fatty acids, in addition to being rich in high-quality protein, B vitamins, and minerals. Cod also contains significant amounts of the B vitamin niacin, important for keeping cholesterol levels in check.

Cooking spray

2 medium tomatoes, diced

3 tablespoons chopped
   fresh thyme

2 teaspoons chopped
   fresh oregano

1 tablespoon minced garlic

2 teaspoons extra-virgin olive oil

4 (4- to 6-ounce) cod filets

2 cups sliced summer squash

Freshly ground black pepper

1. Preheat the oven to 350°F. Lightly coat a 9-by-13-inch baking pan with cooking spray.

2. In a small bowl, combine the tomato, thyme, oregano, and garlic. Add the olive oil and mix well.

3. Arrange the cod filets and squash slices in the baking pan. Spoon the tomato mixture over the fish. Lightly spray the squash with cooking spray and season with freshly ground black pepper.

4. Bake until the fish is opaque throughout when tested with the tip of a knife, 10 to 15 minutes.

5. Transfer one filet and ¼ of the squash to each of 4 serving plates and serve immediately.

Tip: You can switch up the flavor by using fresh basil in place of the thyme. Use your favorite vegetable in place of the summer squash.

Storage: You can store the cooked fish and salsa in an airtight container in the refrigerator for 3 to 4 days. You can also freeze the cod and salsa in airtight containers or heavy-duty freezer bags for 2 to 3 months.

PER SERVING Calories: 233; Total Fat 4g; Saturated Fat: 1g; Cholesterol: 94mg; Sodium: 141mg; Potassium: 810mg; Total Carbohydrate: 8g; Fiber: 3g; Protein: 39g

Cabbage-Stuffed Flounder

Serves 4 / Prep time: 5 minutes / Cook time: 10 minutes

This low-sodium, protein-rich fish recipe includes a serving of fiber and nutritious cabbage in each portion. A very low-calorie, low-fat fish, flounder (or sole) contains beneficial omega-3 fatty acids associated with a lower risk of heart disease. Serve with your favorite whole grain or crusty whole grain bread and a green salad.

Cooking spray

2 teaspoons extra-virgin olive oil

4 cups shredded cabbage

½ cup sliced mushrooms

1 tablespoon minced garlic

Freshly ground black pepper

4 (5- to 6-ounce) flounder
(sole) fillets

1 teaspoon butter

1. Preheat the oven to 400°F. Lightly coat a baking dish with cooking spray.

2. In a medium skillet, heat the olive oil over medium heat. Add the cabbage, mushrooms, garlic, and black pepper and sauté until the cabbage begins to wilt, 2 to 3 minutes.

3. Place the flounder fillets in the prepared baking dish. Place ¼ of the cabbage mixture in the middle of each fillet and roll up. Arrange the rolled fillets seam-side down in the baking dish. Brush with melted butter.

4. Bake until the fish is opaque throughout when tested with the tip of a knife, 8 to 10 minutes.

5. Transfer to individual plates and serve immediately.

Tip: Whether baking, broiling, grilling, or poaching fish, cook for 8 to 10 minutes per 1-inch thickness, measured at the thickest point. Test for doneness at the earliest time given to prevent the fish from overcooking and losing its moist texture.

Storage: You can store cooked fish in an airtight container in the refrigerator for 3 to 4 days. You can also freeze the fish in airtight containers or heavy-duty freezer bags for 2 to 3 months.

PER SERVING Calories: 185; Total Fat 5g; Saturated Fat: 1g; Cholesterol: 100mg; Sodium: 134mg; Potassium: 208mg; Total Carbohydrate: 5g; Fiber: 2g; Protein: 31g

Pan Seared Salmon with Balsamic-Rosemary Roasted Vegetables

Serves 4 / Prep time: 10 minutes / Cook time: 25 to 30 minutes

This delicious seared salmon recipe is great for beginners. The trick to getting a nice crust on fish while ensuring it doesn't stick to the pan is to make sure your skillet is very hot before adding the fish. With ample protein and heart-healthy omega-3 fatty acids, this recipe also provides a hefty four servings of vegetables per portion.

1 large sweet potato, peeled and cubed

1 red bell pepper, cut into bite-size pieces

1 cup Brussels sprouts, trimmed and halved

2 tablespoons extra-virgin olive oil, divided

1 tablespoon balsamic vinegar

2 teaspoons fresh rosemary

Freshly ground black pepper

3 cups baby spinach leaves

2 (6-ounce) skinless, boneless salmon fillets

2 teaspoons ground rosemary

Freshly ground black pepper

1. Preheat the oven to 400°F.

2. Toss the sweet potato, bell pepper, and Brussels sprouts with the olive oil and vinegar, and lay on a sheet pan in a single layer. Season with fresh rosemary and black pepper.

3. Roast until tender, 25 to 30 minutes.

4. While the vegetables are cooking, if the salmon has been in the fridge, allow it to sit at room temperature for about 10 minutes. Season the fillets with ground rosemary and black pepper.

5. Heat a large skillet over medium high heat and let it sit for about 5 minutes until very hot. Add the olive oil and swirl to coat the bottom of the pan. Add the salmon and cook until it lifts easily with a spatula and is well browned, about 3 minutes.

6. Flip and cook until the salmon is nearly opaque in the center, about 1 minute more. Transfer the salmon to a plate.

7. When the vegetables are roasted, remove the pan from the oven and immediately add the spinach to the hot pan. Stir with a spatula until the vegetables are tossed and the spinach is wilted.

8. Serve the salmon on top of the vegetables.

Tip: Squeezing fresh lemon on fish neutralizes any strong fish odors, improving the taste of the fish.

Storage: You can store the cooked salmon and vegetables in an airtight container in the refrigerator for 3 to 4 days. You can also freeze the salmon and vegetables in airtight containers or heavy-duty freezer bags for 2 to 3 months.

PER SERVING Calories: 263; Total Fat 14g; Saturated Fat: 3g; Cholesterol: 43mg; Sodium: 74mg; Potassium: 259mg; Total Carbohydrate: 15g; Fiber: 3g; Protein: 20g

Roasted Salmon with Spinach-Quinoa Salad

Serves 2 / Prep time: 5 minutes / Cook time: 15 minutes

This easy and delicious recipe uses heart-healthy salmon served with a quick-to-prepare spinach and quinoa salad. Full of high-quality protein, fiber, and vitamins and minerals, grapes add a naturally tart flavor and boost of antioxidants to finish the salad.

FOR THE SALMON

Cooking spray

2 (6-ounce) boneless, skinless
    salmon fillets

2 teaspoons extra-virgin olive oil

⅛ teaspoon freshly ground
    black pepper

2 cups baby spinach

½ cup cooked quinoa

12 seedless red grapes, halved

FOR THE DRESSING

2 tablespoons extra-virgin olive oil

2 tablespoons freshly squeezed
    lemon juice

1 tablespoon no-salt stone-
    ground mustard

1 teaspoon minced garlic

Pinch freshly ground black pepper

TO MAKE THE SALMON

1. Preheat the oven to 425°F. Line a baking sheet with aluminum foil and coat with cooking spray.

2. Place the salmon on the prepared baking sheet and rub evenly with the olive oil. Season with the black pepper.

3. Bake for 10 minutes or until fish flakes easily with a fork.

4. While the fish cooks, in a medium bowl, combine the spinach, quinoa, and grapes and toss to combine.

TO MAKE THE DRESSING

1. In a small bowl, whisk together the olive oil, lemon juice, mustard, garlic, and black pepper.

2. Add the dressing to the spinach mixture and toss to combine. Let stand 5 minutes.

3. Divide the salad between serving plates and top with the salmon.

Tip: You can substitute thinly-sliced lacinato kale for the spinach if desired.

Storage: You can store the cooked salmon and salad in separate airtight containers in the refrigerator for 3 to 4 days. You can also freeze the salmon and salad without dressing in separate airtight containers or heavy-duty freezer bags for 2 to 3 months.

PER SERVING Calories: 572; Total Fat 34g; Saturated Fat: 7g; Cholesterol: 85mg; Sodium: 107mg; Potassium: 150mg; Total Carbohydrate: 30g; Fiber: 3g; Protein: 40g

Fish Tacos with Mango Salsa

Serves 4 / Prep time: 10 minutes / Cook time: 8 minutes

Making fish tacos at home doesn't have to be a complicated affair. The fish for this recipe is simple to prepare, taking just minutes to cook on the stove top. The cooked fish is mixed with a freshly-prepared mango salsa and wrapped in lettuce leaves for a fast, easy, nutritious, and delicious weeknight meal.

1 mango, diced
2 plum tomatoes, chopped
1 small red onion, chopped
½ jalapeño, seeded and diced
¼ cup chopped fresh cilantro
Juice of 2 limes
Freshly ground black pepper

1 tablespoon extra-virgin olive oil
12 ounces snapper, sole, tilapia, rockfish, or catfish fillets
12 romaine lettuce leaves
1 avocado, peeled, seeded, and sliced

1. Combine the mango, tomatoes, onion, jalapeño, cilantro, and lime juice in a medium mixing bowl and season with black pepper.

2. Heat the olive oil in a large, heavy pan over medium-high heat until the oil shimmers. Add the fish to the pan, arranging it in a single layer with a little space in between.

3. Cook until both sides are golden-brown, carefully flipping once with a spatula, until the fish is opaque and flakes apart easily in the thickest part, 2 to 3 minutes per side.

4. Transfer the fish to a plate and flake into large chunks.

5. Add the fish to the mango salsa and fold carefully. Divide the mixture between the lettuce leaves and roll.

6. Serve topped with avocado slices.

Tip: You can also serve the tacos with warmed flour or corn tortillas if desired.

Storage: You can store the cooked fish and mango salsa in separate airtight containers in the refrigerator for 3 to 4 days. You can also freeze the fish and salsa in separate airtight containers or heavy-duty freezer bags for 2 to 3 months.

PER SERVING Calories: 268; Total Fat 12g; Saturated Fat: 2g; Cholesterol: 40mg; Sodium: 60mg; Potassium: 971mg; Total Carbohydrate: 16g; Fiber: 5g; Protein: 24g

Shrimp and Black Bean Salad

Serves 4 / Prep time: 20 minutes

This quick and easy no-cook recipe is loaded with fiber- and protein-rich black beans, fresh vegetables, and low-calorie, high-protein shrimp. With the flavors of freshly made salsa, this one-dish recipe can be made one day in advance and served as is, or with fresh corn tortillas.

¼ cup cider vinegar

2 tablespoons extra-virgin olive oil

1 tablespoon minced chipotle chiles in adobo sauce

1 teaspoon ground cumin

1 pound cooked shrimp, peeled and deveined, cut into ½ inch pieces

1 (15-ounce) can black beans, drained and rinsed

1 cup quartered cherry tomatoes

1 bell pepper, chopped

½ cup corn

¼ cup chopped green onion

¼ cup chopped fresh cilantro

1 avocado, peeled, seeded, and sliced

1. In a large bowl, whisk together the vinegar, olive oil, chipotle chiles, and cumin.

2. Add the shrimp, beans, tomatoes, bell pepper, corn, green onion, and cilantro, tossing to coat.

3. Serve cold with the avocado slices.

Tip: Chipotle chiles in adobo sauce are smoked jalapeños in a flavorful sauce. Look for small cans with the Mexican foods at large supermarkets. Once opened, they'll keep for up to 2 weeks in the refrigerator or 6 months in the freezer.

Storage: The shrimp salad can be stored in the refrigerator in an airtight container for 3 to 4 days. It can also be frozen and stored in airtight containers or heavy-duty freezer bags for 3 to 4 months.

PER SERVING Calories: 390; Total Fat 16g; Saturated Fat: 2g; Cholesterol: 172mg; Sodium: 245mg; Potassium: 623mg; Total Carbohydrate: 32g; Fiber: 9g; Protein: 31g

Shrimp Jambalaya

Serves 6 / Prep time: 15 minutes / Cook time: 20 to 30 minutes

Jambalaya is a one-pot main dish from Louisiana consisting of meat—often chicken, sausage, and/or shrimp—and vegetables with rice and stock simmered together before serving. This simple shrimp and rice recipe is inspired by traditional recipes, but it is healthier and lower in sodium due to the use of more nutrient- and fiber-rich veggies and the omission of sausage.

2 tablespoons extra-virgin olive oil
1 cup chopped red onion
½ cup chopped celery
½ cup chopped green bell pepper
3 cups low sodium chicken broth
1 ½ cups uncooked long grain rice

2 teaspoons no-salt Creole seasoning
1/8 teaspoon cayenne pepper
1 pound cooked medium shrimp, peeled and deveined
1 cup cherry tomatoes, halved
½ cup chopped green onion

1. Heat the olive oil in a large skillet over medium-high heat. Add the onion, celery, and bell pepper and sauté until tender, 3 to 5 minutes. Add the broth, rice, Creole seasoning, and cayenne.

2. Bring to a boil. Reduce heat to low, cover, and cook until rice is tender, 15 to 20 minutes.

3. Stir in the shrimp, tomatoes, and green onion and heat through. Serve immediately.

Tip: You can substitute ¼ teaspoon each garlic powder and paprika, and 1/8 teaspoon each dried thyme, ground cumin, and cayenne pepper for the Creole seasoning.

Storage: Store in an airtight container in the refrigerator for 3 to 4 days.

PER SERVING Calories: 320; Total Fat 6g; Saturated Fat: 1g; Cholesterol: 115mg; Sodium: 163mg; Potassium: 338mg; Total Carbohydrate: 43g; Fiber: 2g; Protein: 20g

Chili and Red Pepper–Crusted Scallops

Serves: 4 / Prep time: 10 minutes / Cook time: 5 minutes

Scallops are a very delicately flavored shellfish that are as versatile as shrimp. They cook quickly, so be sure to not overcook them or they will dry out. These taste delicious paired with fresh greens or over rice.

¼ cup chili powder

2 tablespoons ground
toasted cumin

1 teaspoon freshly ground
black pepper

¼ cup extra-virgin olive oil

12 sea scallops, rinsed and
patted dry

1. In a medium, shallow bowl combine the chili powder, cumin, and black pepper.

2. Heat the olive oil in a large sauté pan over medium high heat until smoking. While the oil is heating, dip one side of each scallop into the spice mixture.

3. Place the scallops in the heated pan, spice mixture-side down, and cook for 20 seconds.

4. Reduce the heat to low, flip the scallops and cook for 2 to 3 minutes more.

PER SERVING Calories: 244; Total Fat 16g; Saturated Fat: 2g; Cholesterol: 35mg; Sodium: 236mg; Potassium: 150mg; Total Carbohydrate: 7g; Fiber: 3g; Protein: 18g

Lemon Pepper Salmon in Foil

Serves: 2 / Prep time: 5 minutes / Cook time: 10 minutes

Foil packets are great for cooking at home or at the cabin. The best part is that they can be prepared ahead of time and frozen for use throughout the week. They thaw and cook quickly for an easy dinner option.

2 teaspoons butter, divided

4 thin slices lemon

⅛ teaspoon sugar, divided

2 (4- to 6-ounce) salmon fillets

⅛ teaspoon freshly ground
    black pepper

⅛ teaspoon pinch dill

⅛ teaspoon pinch chopped parsley,
    fresh or dried (optional)

½ lemon

1. Preheat the oven to 425°F.

2. Use 1 teaspoon butter to grease two 12-by-12-inch squares of aluminum foil, leaving an ungreased 2 inch border all around.

3. Place 2 lemon slices, off-center, on each foil square, and sprinkle with a pinch of sugar each.

4. Place the salmon on the lemon slices and season with black pepper, dill, and parsley (if using). Lightly squeeze the lemon over each filet.

5. Fold the foil over the fish, then fold the ends together to seal each packet.

6. Place the foil packets on the baking sheet and bake for 10 minutes.

7. Open the foil packet, being careful to avoid the steam being released, and check that the fish is cooked. It should flake easily with a fork. Serve immediately.

PER SERVING Calories: 320; Total Fat 19g; Saturated Fat: 7g; Cholesterol: 97mg; Sodium: 72mg; Potassium: 82mg; Total Carbohydrate: 6g; Fiber: 3g; Protein: 36g

Greek Fish in a Packet

Serves 2 / Prep time: 10 minutes / Cook time: 20 minutes

This one-pan quick and easy fish dish includes thin slices of fennel bulb, a versatile winter-season vegetable native to the Mediterranean. Fennel bulb has numerous health benefits that support heart health including cholesterol-lowering fiber, potassium, folate, vitamin C, vitamin B_6 and numerous health-promoting phytochemicals. Serve this no-fuss meal with brown rice, couscous, or orzo.

2 tablespoons extra-virgin olive oil, plus more for brushing

2 (5- to 6-ounce) haddock fillets (or other firm fish)

1 cup thinly-sliced fennel bulb

2 small tomatoes, sliced

8 thin slices red onion

Juice of 1 lemon

2 garlic cloves, minced

1 tablespoon chopped fresh dill

Pinch freshly ground black pepper

1. Preheat the oven to 450°F.

2. Fold two sheets of 12-by-24-inch aluminum foil over to make a double-thick square. Brush a little olive oil in the center of each square.

3. Rinse the fish.

4. Layer half of the fennel, tomatoes, and onion on each foil square. Top each with one fish fillet.

5. In a cup, combine the 2 tablespoons olive oil, the garlic, lemon juice, and dill and pour over the fish. Season lightly with the black pepper.

6. Fold the foil over the fish, then fold the ends together to seal each packet. Bake for 20 minutes.

7. Place the foil packets on a plate, and, being careful to avoid the steam that will be released, open the foil and check that the fish is cooked. It should flake easily with a fork.

8. Using a spatula, transfer the fish and vegetables to individual serving plates and pour the collected liquid in the foil packet over each serving.

Storage: The cooked haddock and vegetables can be stored in an airtight container in the refrigerator for 3 to 4 days. It can also be frozen in an airtight container or heavy-duty freezer bag for 2 to 3 months.

PER SERVING Calories: 378; Total Fat 16g; Saturated Fat: 2g; Cholesterol: 126mg; Sodium: 177mg; Potassium: 1041mg; Total Carbohydrate: 15g; Fiber: 4g; Protein: 45g

Pork Chops with Tomato and Fennel p.178

10

MEAT AND POULTRY ENTRÉES

SODIUM

LOWEST

DAIRY-FREE
GLUTEN-FREE
LOW-FAT
ONE-POT

Slow-Cooker Hawaiian Chicken

Serves 5 / Prep time: 15 minutes / Cook time: 4 to 5 hours on low

This Hawaiian chicken slow-cooker recipe is a flavorful, light blend of sweet and savory. Serve the chicken in collard leaves, on a bed of greens, on top of a sweet potato, or over cauliflower rice. This recipe can be served hot or cold.

1 pound boneless, skinless
   chicken breasts
1 small onion, diced
4 garlic cloves, minced
1 (8-ounce) can crushed pineapple,
   undrained
¼ cup water
Juice of 1 lime

1 teaspoon ground ginger
¼ teaspoon red pepper flakes
¼ teaspoon freshly ground
   black pepper
Collard leaves (or lettuce)
   for wrapping
Sliced avocado, shredded carrots,
   fresh cilantro, for toppings

1. Add the chicken breasts, onion, and garlic to a slow cooker.

2. In a small bowl, combine the pineapple and its liquid, the water, lime juice, ginger, red pepper flakes, and black pepper. Add this mixture to the slow cooker.

3. Cook on low for 4 to 5 hours. Remove the chicken from the slow cooker and shred with two forks.

4. Return the chicken to the slow cooker, stir to mix all ingredients, and set the temperature to low until ready to serve.

5. Spoon the chicken mixture into the collard leaves, add desired toppings, wrap, and enjoy.

Tip: Prep the collard leaves by shaving the thick stems that run down the center of the leaves, which makes them more flexible for wrapping. An additional optional step is to blanch them for 30 seconds in boiling water followed by soaking in an ice bath.

Storage: You can store leftover cooked chicken in the refrigerator in an airtight container for 3 to 4 days. You can also freeze it in airtight containers or heavy-duty freezer bags for up to 4 months.

PER SERVING Calories: 164; Total Fat 3g; Saturated Fat: 1g; Cholesterol: 52mg; Sodium: 40mg; Potassium: 120mg; Total Carbohydrate: 11g; Fiber: 2g; Protein: 22g

Slow-Cooker Turkey Quinoa Meatballs

Serves 6 / Prep time: 30 minutes / Cook time: 6 hours on low

This low-fat turkey meatball recipe uses high-fiber, nutrient-rich quinoa in place of less nutritious breadcrumbs. These mini-meatballs are sure to be a hit served with roasted vegetables, a green salad, or your favorite sides.

1 pound 99 percent lean ground turkey breast

1 pound 93 percent lean ground turkey

1 cup cooked quinoa

4 garlic cloves, minced

1 large egg, lightly beaten

2½ tablespoons extra-virgin olive oil, divided

2 teaspoons dried basil

1 teaspoon dried oregano

1 teaspoon onion powder

½ teaspoon freshly ground black pepper

1 large sweet onion, sliced into thin rounds

2 (28-ounce) cans no-salt crushed tomatoes

1. In a large bowl, combine the ground turkey, quinoa, garlic, egg, 2 tablespoons of the olive oil, the basil, oregano, onion powder, and black pepper. Mix thoroughly but quickly, just so the ingredients are combined.

2. Roll into 40-50 mini-meatballs slightly smaller than a golf ball, and place on a baking sheet.

3. Layer sliced onion on the bottom of a slow cooker and add 1 can of crushed tomatoes.

4. In a large skillet over medium-high heat, heat the remaining ½ tablespoon of olive oil. Add the meatballs, searing on the top and bottom until golden, about 1 minute per side.

5. One at a time, place the meatballs in the slow cooker, stacking them. Top with the other can of crushed tomatoes, completely submerging the meatballs.

6. Cover and cook on low for 6 hours. Serve.

Tip: The browning step helps seal the juices in so the meatballs hold together and are tender.

Storage: You can store the cooked meatballs in an airtight container in the refrigerator for 3 to 4 days. You can also freeze them in an airtight container or heavy-duty freezer bag for 3 to 4 months.

PER SERVING Calories: 352; Total Fat 14g; Saturated Fat: 3g; Cholesterol: 121mg; Sodium: 219mg; Potassium: 138mg; Total Carbohydrate: 22g; Fiber: 6g; Protein: 37g

Slow-Cooker Apple Pork Loin

SODIUM

LOWER

DAIRY-FREE
GLUTEN-FREE
LOW-FAT
ONE-POT

Serves 6 / Prep time: 10 minutes / Cook time: 6 hours on low

This slow-cooker combination of pork, cinnamon, honey, and apples delivers a delicious and satisfying meal perfect for fall. Pork tenderloin is a lean protein source packed with B vitamins and essential minerals important for health, making it a healthy choice to include in your diet. Serve this dish with a green salad.

1 (2- to 3-pound) boneless
   pork tenderloin
2 teaspoons cinnamon, divided
½ teaspoon freshly ground
   black pepper
¼ teaspoon ground nutmeg
3 apples, cored and sliced
   (peel left on)

¼ cup apple cider, 100 percent
   apple juice, or water
4 tablespoons honey
6 baby red potatoes
2 Vidalia onions, peeled and
   left whole
2 celery stalks, sliced

1. Cut slits about ½- to-1-inch deep across the top of the pork loin. Sprinkle all sides of the loin and inside the slits with the 1 teaspoon of the cinnamon, the salt, black pepper, and nutmeg.

2. Scatter a few apple slices in the bottom of a slow cooker and pour in the apple cider. Place the pork loin on top of apples.

3. Drizzle honey into each slit and all over the top of the loin; place an apple slice in each slit.

4. Fit the remaining apples slices, potatoes, onions, and celery around and on top of the pork loin. Sprinkle with remaining 1 teaspoon cinnamon.

5. Cook on low for 6 hours. Serve.

Tip: An optional step is to heat 2 tablespoons extra-virgin olive oil in a large Dutch oven over medium-high heat. Place the pork loin in the Dutch oven and brown on all sides prior to placing in the slow cooker. Browning adds color and more depth of flavor.

Storage: You can store the cooked pork tenderloin in an airtight covered container in the refrigerator for 3 to 4 days. You can also freeze leftovers in an airtight container or heavy-duty freezer bags for 2 to 3 months.

PER SERVING Calories: 285; Total Fat 4g; Saturated Fat: 1g; Cholesterol: 60mg; Sodium: 88mg; Potassium: 346mg; Total Carbohydrate: 33g; Fiber: 4g; Protein: 32g

Slow-Cooker Bison Tacos

Serves 6 / Prep time: 10 minutes / Cook time: 4 hours on low

Bison provides a leaner protein source than cattle, so you may want to consider choosing it for its many health benefits. Bison is lower in total fat and contains higher levels of heart-healthy omega-3 fatty acids than beef, which can help lower your risk of heart disease. This recipe is super-versatile and can be used in tacos, salads, egg scrambles, and more.

1½ pounds ground bison

½ cup chopped onion

2 teaspoons chili powder

1 teaspoon dried oregano

1 teaspoon ground cumin

1 teaspoon garlic powder

¼ teaspoon ground paprika

¼ teaspoon cayenne pepper (optional)

3 ounces no-salt tomato paste (half of a 6-ounce can)

1 head romaine, butter, red or green leaf lettuce

1 cup shredded carrots, for serving

Fresh cilantro, for garnish

1. Add the bison, onion, chili powder, oregano, cumin, garlic powder, paprika, cayenne (if using), and tomato paste to a slow cooker. Use a large spoon to break up the meat and mix in the tomato paste and spices.

2. Cover and cook on low for 4 hours. After 1 hour, stir. Cover and continue to cook for 3 hours more, stirring as needed.

3. Serve in lettuce wraps, topped with shredded carrots and cilantro.

Tip: You can boost the vegetable content of this recipe by adding 1 to 2 cups of your favorite chopped vegetables such as bell pepper, zucchini, or carrot. You could also add cubed sweet potato for a heartier dish.

Storage: You can store the cooked bison meat in an airtight container in the refrigerator for 3 to 4 days. Bison meat can also be frozen in airtight containers or heavy-duty freezer bags for 2 to 3 months.

PER SERVING Calories: 302; Total Fat 18g; Saturated Fat: 7g; Cholesterol: 94mg; Sodium: 122mg; Potassium: 700mg; Total Carbohydrate: 7g; Fiber: 2g; Protein: 28g

Slow-Cooker Shredded Root Beer Beef

Serves 10 / Prep time: 15 minutes / Cook time: 8 to 10 hours on low

SODIUM
LOW

DAIRY-FREE
GLUTEN-FREE
ONE-POT

I find this to be an excellent weekend dish. If you're tailgating or cooking for a game, have extra buns because the beef makes the perfect slider filling. You can substitute pork for the beef if you prefer.

1 (4-pound) beef butt roast

1 (12-ounce) can or bottle root beer

4 ounces liquid smoke

4 garlic cloves

1. Place the butt roast in a slow cooker and pour the root beer and liquid smoke over the top. Top with the garlic.

2. Cover and cook on low for 8 to 10 hours.

3. Transfer the roast to a bowl, then strain the liquid through a fine-mesh sieve, discarding the liquid.

4. Add the softened garlic to the beef and shred the beef using two forks.

PER SERVING Calories: 346; Total Fat 18g; Saturated Fat: 7g; Cholesterol: 88mg; Sodium: 360mg; Potassium: 5mg; Total Carbohydrate: 5g; Fiber: 0g; Protein: 35g

Slow-Cooker Sweet and Sour Chicken

Serves: 4 / Prep time: 15 minutes
Cook time 2 hours and 30 minutes on high, 4 hours and 30 minutes on low

This recipe is a great base to add other flavors for a fresh taste each time you make it. Here I add pineapple, but you can add papaya or mango with the pineapple, or add unsalted nuts like cashews or peanuts. Sesame or pumpkin seeds work nicely as well. Serve over a bed of rice or egg noodles.

1 egg, beaten

½ cup all-purpose flour

1 pound chicken thighs or breasts, cut into bite-size pieces

1 tablespoon coconut oil (or oil of preference)

1 (6-ounce) can tomato paste

½ cup water

2 tablespoons apple cider vinegar

2 tablespoons brown sugar

2 tablespoons freshly grated ginger

1 small red onion, diced

1 bell pepper, diced

1 head broccoli, cut into florets

1 ½ cups fresh pineapple, diced

1. Put the egg and flour in separate, flat-bottomed bowls.

2. Dip the chicken pieces into the egg, and dredge in the flour.

3. Heat the oil in a large pan over medium-high heat. Add the chicken and brown, about 20 to 30 seconds per side. Set aside.

4. Add the tomato paste, water, vinegar, sugar, and ginger to a slow cooker and mix to combine.

5. Add the onion, bell pepper, broccoli, and pineapple and stir. Top with the chicken and stir until all ingredients are coated with sauce.

6. Cover and cook on low for 4½ hours or on high for 2½ hours.

PER SERVING Calories: 387; Total Fat 13g; Saturated Fat: 6g; Cholesterol: 112mg; Sodium: 498mg; Potassium: 1089mg; Total Carbohydrate: 44g; Fiber: 9g; Protein: 31g

Slow-Cooker Curry Chicken

Serves 4 / Prep time: 20 minutes / Cook time: 4 to 5 hours on high, 6 to 7 hours on low

This simple and delicious curried chicken can be assembled in minutes. Lean, high-quality protein chicken is slow cooked with Indian spices and cauliflower, onions, and golden raisins. Loaded with flavor, not sodium, serve this dish over basmati rice and top with fresh cilantro.

1 (15-ounce) can no-salt diced tomatoes

2 tablespoons tomato paste

2 tablespoons freshly grated ginger

1 tablespoon curry powder

¼ teaspoon freshly ground black pepper

1½ pounds boneless, skinless chicken breast

4 cups cauliflower florets

1 medium onion, sliced

¼ cup golden raisins

½ cup chopped fresh cilantro

1. In a 5 to 6 quart slow cooker, whisk together the tomatoes, tomato paste, ginger, curry powder, and black pepper.

2. Add the chicken, cauliflower, onion, and raisins and stir to combine.

3. Cook, covered, until chicken is cooked through, 4 to 5 hours on high, or 6 to 7 hours on low.

4. Top with chopped fresh cilantro.

Storage: You can store the curry in the refrigerator in an airtight container for 3 to 4 days. You can also freeze it in an airtight container or heavy-duty freezer bag for up to 3 months.

PER SERVING Calories: 313; Total Fat 7g; Saturated Fat: 2g; Cholesterol: 98mg; Sodium: 209mg; Potassium: 535mg; Total Carbohydrate: 24g; Fiber: 6g; Protein: 42g

Slow-Cooker Southwest Chicken

Serves 6 / Prep time: 10 minutes / Cook time: 8 to 10 hours on low, 3 to 4 hours on high

This heart-healthy slow-cooker recipe uses lean chicken breast with Southwest seasonings to create a flavorful, yet low-sodium meal. Made with a few pantry staples, this no-fuss recipe is extremely versatile and can be served with beans, on lettuce, or in whole wheat tortillas.

2 teaspoons chili powder

1 teaspoon cumin

1 teaspoon paprika

¼ teaspoon oregano

¼ to ½ teaspoon cayenne pepper (optional)

1 pound boneless, skinless chicken breasts

1 green bell pepper, chopped

1 medium onion, diced

2 garlic cloves, minced

½ teaspoon freshly ground black pepper

1 (14.5-ounce) can no-salt-added, diced tomatoes, undrained

1 (3-ounce) can green chilies

1 cup low-sodium chicken broth

1. In a small bowl, stir together chili powder, cumin, paprika, oregano, and cayenne (if using).

2. Add the chicken to a slow cooker and sprinkle half of the seasoning mixture over. Flip the chicken with a fork and sprinkle with the remaining half of seasoning mixture.

3. Place the bell pepper, onion, garlic, black pepper, tomatoes, and chilies over the chicken and pour the chicken broth on top.

4. Cover and cook on low for 8 to 10 hours, or on high for 3 to 4 hours. The chicken will break apart easily with a fork once cooked.

Tip: If you are short on time, replace the onion with ½ to 1 teaspoon no-salt onion powder and the garlic cloves with ½ to 1 teaspoon no-salt garlic powder.

Storage: You can store leftover cooked chicken in the refrigerator in an airtight container for 3 to 4 days. You can also freeze it in airtight containers or heavy-duty freezer bags for up to 4 months.

PER SERVING Calories: 133; Total Fat 3g; Saturated Fat: 1g; Cholesterol: 43mg; Sodium: 85mg; Potassium: 107mg; Total Carbohydrate: 8g; Fiber: 2g; Protein: 18g

Slow-Cooker Lemon-Garlic Chicken

Serves 6 / Prep time: 10 minutes / Cook time: 3 hours on high, 6 hours on low

This juicy and moist recipe for lemon-garlic chicken is low in sodium yet full of flavor. To lock in flavor, lean chicken breast is seasoned and quickly pan-seared before being placed in a slow cooker. Serve this simple dish with your favorite grains and steamed vegetables.

1 teaspoon dried oregano

¼ teaspoon freshly ground black pepper

2 pounds skinless, boneless chicken breast

1 tablespoon extra-virgin olive oil

¼ cup low-sodium chicken broth

3 tablespoons freshly squeezed lemon juice

2 teaspoons garlic, minced

¼ cup chopped fresh parsley

1. In a small bowl, mix together the oregano and black pepper.

2. Sprinkle the mixture evenly over the chicken.

3. In a large, nonstick skillet over medium heat, heat the olive oil. Add the chicken and brown on both sides, about 3 minutes per side. Place the chicken pieces in a slow cooker.

4. Add the broth, lemon juice, and garlic to the skillet and bring mixture to a gentle boil.

5. Pour the lemon juice mixture over the chicken in the slow cooker and cover.

6. Cook on high for 3 hours or on low for 6 hours. Sprinkle the parsley on top of the chicken about 15 to 30 minutes before the end of cooking time. Serve.

Tip: If you have no-salt lemon pepper seasoning, you can use ½ teaspoon of that instead of the black pepper. Just subtract 1 tablespoon lemon juice and increase the water by 1 tablespoon.

Storage: You can store leftover cooked chicken in the refrigerator in an airtight container for 3 to 4 days. You can also freeze it in airtight containers or heavy-duty freezer bags for up to 4 months.

PER SERVING Calories: 212; Total Fat 8g; Saturated Fat: 2g; Cholesterol: 87mg; Sodium: 60mg; Potassium: 31mg; Total Carbohydrate: 1g; Fiber: 0g; Protein: 34g

Slow-Cooker Pork Chops and Potatoes

Serves 4 / Prep time: 10 minutes / Cook time: 6 to 8 hours on low, 3 to 4 hours on high

Most methods of preparing pork chops require the generous use of salt to keep them moist. Using a slow cooker eliminates needing salt through the use of a slower cook time using a low-sodium broth. The addition of potatoes, onions, and vegetables creates a one-pot meal ready to serve with a simple side salad.

1 cup diced onion

4 small sweet potatoes, cut into chunks

1 (10.5-ounce) can low sodium chicken broth (about 1⅓ cups)

1 cup broccoli florets

1 cup sliced carrot

4 boneless, skinless pork chops

1. Layer the onion and sweet potatoes at the bottom of a slow cooker.

2. Pour half of the chicken broth over the potatoes and onions.

3. Place the pork chops on top of onions and potatoes then top with the broccoli and carrot. Pour the remaining chicken broth on top.

4. Cover and cook on low for 6 to 8 hours or on high for 3 to 4 hours.

Tip: You can substitute red potatoes or gold potatoes for the sweet potatoes if you like.

Storage: You can store leftover pork chops in the refrigerator in an airtight container for 3 to 4 days. You can also freeze the cooked meat in an airtight container or heavy-duty freezer bag for 2 to 3 months.

PER SERVING Calories: 316; Total Fat 7g; Saturated Fat: 3g; Cholesterol: 45mg; Sodium: 319mg; Potassium: 502mg; Total Carbohydrate: 40g; Fiber: 7g; Protein: 25g

New York Strip Steak with Mushroom Sauce

Serves 2 / Prep time: 5 minutes / Cook time: 25 minutes

Strip steak is one of the leanest cuts you can choose, and because it comes from a part of the animal that doesn't move a lot, this cut is very tender. Remember to keep portions in check.

Cooking spray

2 (4-ounce) New York strip steaks, trimmed of all visible fat

2 teaspoons extra-virgin olive oil

3 garlic cloves

4 ounces sliced shitake mushrooms

4 ounces button mushrooms

½ teaspoon thyme

¼ teaspoon rosemary

¼ cup balsamic vinegar

¼ cup white wine

Freshly ground black pepper

1. Heat the gas grill or broiler. Away from the heat source, lightly coat a grill rack or broiler pan with cooking spray. Position the cooking rack 4 to 6 inches from the heat source.

2. Grill or broil the steaks until a food thermometer reads 160°F (medium) or 170°F (well done), about 10 minutes per side.

3. Meanwhile, heat the olive oil in a small saucepan over medium heat. Add the garlic, mushrooms, thyme, and rosemary and sauté until the mushrooms are tender, about 1 to 2 minutes.

4. Add the balsamic vinegar and wine, and season with black pepper. Continue to cook, stirring, for another 1 to 2 minutes.

5. Top the steaks with the mushroom mixture and serve immediately.

Storage: You can store cooked steaks in the refrigerator in an airtight container for 3 to 4 days. You can also freeze the steaks in heavy-duty freezer bags for 2 to 3 months.

PER SERVING Calories: 334; Total Fat 19g; Saturated Fat: 6g; Cholesterol: 75mg; Sodium: 24mg; Potassium: 47mg; Total Carbohydrate: 11g; Fiber: 2g; Protein: 27g

Chimichurri Skirt Steak

Serves 2 to 3 / Prep time: 5 minutes / Cook time: 4 minutes, plus overnight

Chimichurri sauce is delicious with a variety of proteins—it will enhance fish, chicken, or pork dishes just as well as beef. This is more of a rustic sauce, so don't over puree it.

FOR THE CHIMICHURRI SAUCE

1 cup fresh parsley leaves,
  tightly packed

1 tablespoon fresh oregano leaves,
  tightly packed

4 garlic cloves, minced

2 teaspoons red pepper flakes
  (optional)

¼ cup red wine vinegar

Freshly ground black pepper

½ cup extra-virgin olive oil

FOR THE SKIRT STEAK

1 pound skirt steak, at room
  temperature

Freshly ground black pepper

TO MAKE THE CHIMICHURRI SAUCE

1. In a food processor, add the parsley, oregano, garlic, red pepper flakes and red wine vinegar. Blend until finely chopped, but not pureed.

2. Transfer into a small bowl. Add the black pepper and olive oil and stir to combine. You should have about ¾ cup.

TO MAKE THE STEAK

1. Marinate the steak with the chimichurri sauce in a resealable bag overnight.

2. Heat your grill or a heavy skillet over high heat until smoking.

3. Remove the skirt steak from the marinade and sprinkle each side with black pepper.

4. Grill the skirt steak for 2 minutes on each side.

5. Transfer to a plate, cover loosely with foil and rest for 7 to 10 minutes.

6. Cut the steak into thin slices, against the grain.

Tip: Store the chimichurri sauce in an airtight container in the refrigerator and use within 3 days.

PER SERVING Calories: 980; Total Fat 78g; Saturated Fat: 16g; Cholesterol: 134mg; Sodium: 190mg; Potassium: 933mg; Total Carbohydrate: 6g; Fiber: 3g; Protein: 62g

Pork Chops with Tomato and Fennel

Serves 4 / Prep time: 10 minutes / Cook time: 25 minutes

Lean pork chops are a protein-rich meat choice. They are low in calories and fat and rich in heart-healthy B vitamins. The flavorful tomato and fennel sauce reduces the need for added salt. Each portion comes with several servings of vegetables. Serve with a simple side salad.

1 clove garlic, cut in half lengthwise

4 (5-ounce) lean boneless pork chops, visible fat trimmed off

2 tablespoons extra-virgin olive oil, divided

2 fennel bulbs, thinly sliced (about 2 to 3 cups)

1 large onion, thinly sliced

6 garlic cloves, minced

2 (14-ounce) cans no-salt-added diced tomatoes

1½ teaspoons dried oregano

1 teaspoon dried rosemary

½ teaspoon thyme

Freshly ground black pepper

¼ cup chopped fresh basil

1. Rub the cut sides of the garlic halves on both sides of the chops. Heat 1 tablespoon of the olive oil in a large Dutch oven over medium-high heat. Add the pork chops and quickly brown on both sides, 3 to 4 minutes per side. Transfer the chops to a platter to keep warm.

2. To make the sauce, reduce the heat to medium and add the remaining 1 tablespoon olive oil. Add the fennel and onion and sauté for 4 to 5 minutes.

3. Add the garlic and cook for 1 minute more. Add the tomatoes, oregano, rosemary, thyme, and black pepper and bring to a gentle boil.

4. Return the pork chops to the Dutch oven. Cover, reduce heat to low, and cook for 10 minutes.

5. Uncover and continue cooking for an additional 5 minutes, or to desired doneness.

6. Serve garnished with chopped fresh basil.

Storage: Leftover pork chops can be stored in an airtight container in the refrigerator for 3 to 4 days.

PER SERVING Calories: 312; Total Fat 15g; Saturated Fat: 4g; Cholesterol: 56mg; Sodium: 413mg; Potassium: 281mg; Total Carbohydrate: 18g; Fiber: 7g; Protein: 29g

Pork Medallions with Herbes de Provence

Serves 2 / Prep time: 5 minutes / Cook time: 5 to 8 minutes

One of the tricks to staying on track with a low-sodium diet is to stock your pantry with a large variety of herbs and spices. This recipe uses very lean pork medallions seasoned with flavorful *herbes de Provence*, a combination of dried herbs including thyme, marjoram, rosemary, basil, fennel, sage, and lavender. Serve these medallions with steamed asparagus, brown rice, and a fresh green salad.

8 ounces pork tenderloin, trimmed of visible fat and cut crosswise into 6 pieces

1 tablespoon extra-virgin olive oil

1 medium onion, sliced

2 garlic cloves, minced

1 teaspoon herbes de Provence

¼ cup dry white wine

1. Sprinkle the slices of pork with black pepper. Place the pork between 2 sheets of waxed paper and pound with a mallet or roll with a rolling pin until about ¼ inch thick.

2. In a large, nonstick frying pan over medium-high heat, heat the olive oil. Add the onion and garlic and sauté until the onion is translucent, 3 to 5 minutes.

3. Add the pork medallions and cook until browned, 2 to 3 minutes on each side.

4. Remove from heat and sprinkle with the herbes de Provence. Transfer the pork and vegetables to individual plates.

5. Pour the wine into the pan and cook until boiling. Scrape the brown bits from the bottom of the pan. Pour the wine sauce over the pork and serve immediately.

Tip: For a flavor variation, use slices of fennel bulb in place of the onion.

Storage: You can store leftover pork in the refrigerator in an airtight container for 3 to 4 days. You can also freeze the cooked pork in an airtight container or heavy-duty freezer bag for 2 to 3 months.

PER SERVING Calories: 240; Total Fat 12g; Saturated Fat: 6g; Cholesterol: 45mg; Sodium: 40mg; Potassium: 122mg; Total Carbohydrate: 7g; Fiber: 1g; Protein: 20g

Turkey and Wild Rice

Serves 6 / Prep time: 10 minutes / Cook time: 20 to 25 minutes

This quick and easy turkey and rice recipe is low in calories and fat but full of flavor. Made using a handful of pantry staples, this dish provides lean, high-quality protein and several servings of fiber- and nutrient-rich vegetables in each portion.

3 cups water

1½ cups wild rice

1 tablespoon extra-virgin olive oil

1 cup chopped green bell pepper

2 celery stalks, cut into
   1-inch pieces

2 medium carrots cut into
   1-inch pieces

1 yellow onion, finely chopped

4 garlic cloves, minced

1 pound boneless turkey breast,
   cut into 1-inch cubes

1 (14.5-ounce) can no-salt
   stewed tomatoes

1. In a saucepan, bring the water to a boil. Add the rice and stir. Reduce heat, cover and simmer for 20 to 25 minutes.

2. Meanwhile, heat the olive oil in a large skillet over medium-high heat. Add the bell pepper, celery, carrots, onion, and garlic and sauté until tender, 2 to 3 minutes.

3. Add the turkey and continue to sauté for 2 to 3 minutes. Turn the pieces over and continue cooking until the turkey loses its outer pink color, 2 to 3 minutes more.

4. Stir in the tomatoes and cover. Continue to simmer, stirring occasionally, until the turkey is cooked through and an instant-read thermometer registers 160°F.

5. Serve over the hot wild rice.

Tip: You can substitute the wild rice with long grain or short grain brown rice, quinoa, whole wheat couscous, or sweet potatoes.

Storage: You can store leftover turkey in the refrigerator in an airtight container for 3 to 4 days. You can also freeze it in airtight containers or heavy-duty freezer bags for 2 to 3 months.

PER SERVING Calories: 307; Total Fat 11g; Saturated Fat: 0g; Cholesterol: 37mg; Sodium: 402mg; Potassium: 382mg; Total Carbohydrate: 46g; Fiber: 5g; Protein: 19g

Chocolate Chia Seed Pudding p.195

11

DESSERTS

Baked Apples with Cherries and Walnuts

Serves 6 / Prep time: 10 minutes / Cook time: 35 to 40 minutes

Including more fresh fruits in your diet is a healthy habit to incorporate when managing risk for chronic diseases. Apples are an extremely rich source of important antioxidants and cholesterol-lowering fiber, they are available year-round, and they make a delicious baked dessert. This recipe is easy to customize with your favorite dried fruit and nuts.

⅓ cup dried cherries, coarsely chopped

3 tablespoons chopped walnuts

1 tablespoon ground flaxseed meal

1 tablespoon firmly packed brown sugar

1 teaspoon ground cinnamon

⅛ teaspoon nutmeg

6 Golden Delicious apples, about 2 pounds total weight, washed and unpeeled

½ cup 100 percent apple juice

¼ cup water

2 tablespoons dark honey

2 teaspoons extra-virgin olive oil

1. Preheat the oven to 350°F.

2. In a small bowl, toss together the cherries, walnuts, flaxseed meal, brown sugar, cinnamon, and nutmeg until all the ingredients are evenly distributed. Set aside.

3. Working from the stem end, core each apple, stopping ¾ of an inch from the bottom.

4. Gently press the cherries into each apple cavity. Arrange the apples upright in a heavy ovenproof skillet or baking dish just large enough to hold them.

5. Pour the apple juice and water into the pan.

6. Drizzle the honey and oil evenly over the apples, and cover the pan snugly with aluminum foil. Bake until the apples are tender when pierced with a knife, 35 to 40 minutes.

7. Transfer the apples to individual plates and drizzle with the pan juices. Serve warm.

Tip: For a variation, substitute wheat germ for the ground flaxseed meal.

Storage: Store the baked apples in the refrigerator in an airtight container for 3 to 4 days or freeze by wrapping tightly in plastic wrap or aluminum foil and placing in a heavy-duty freezer bag for 3 to 4 months.

PER SERVING Calories: 162; Total Fat 5g; Saturated Fat: 1g; Cholesterol: 0mg; Sodium: 4mg; Potassium: 148mg; Total Carbohydrate: 30g; Fiber: 4g; Protein: 1g

Easy Peach Crumble

Serves 8 / Prep time: 10 minutes / Cook time: 30 minutes

This delicious, very low-sodium dessert uses fresh peaches, whole grain oats, and whole grain flour to create a tasty dessert. This nutritious dish makes a healthy dessert, snack, or breakfast served with Greek yogurt.

8 ripe peaches, peeled, pitted
   and sliced
3 tablespoons freshly squeezed
   lemon juice
½ teaspoon ground cinnamon
¼ teaspoon ground nutmeg

½ cup oat flour
¼ cup packed dark brown sugar
2 tablespoons margarine, cut into
   thin slices
¼ cup quick-cooking oats

1. Preheat the oven to 375°F. Lightly coat a 9-inch pie pan with cooking spray. Arrange peach slices in the prepared pie plate and sprinkle with the lemon juice, cinnamon, and nutmeg.

2. In a small bowl, whisk together the flour and brown sugar. With your fingers, crumble the margarine into the flour-sugar mixture. Add the uncooked oats and stir to mix. Sprinkle the flour mixture over the peaches.

3. Bake until the peaches are soft and the topping is browned, about 30 minutes.

4. Cut into 8 even slices and serve warm.

Tip: Freestone peaches have pits you can easily remove, while clingstone peaches have flesh that clings to the pit. For this recipe, look for freestone peaches.

Storage: Peach cobbler can be stored in the refrigerator in airtight containers for 2 to 3 days. It can also be frozen in airtight containers for 6 to 8 months.

PER SERVING Calories: 130; Total Fat 4g; Saturated Fat: 0g; Cholesterol: 0mg; Sodium: 42mg; Potassium: 255mg; Total Carbohydrate: 28g; Fiber: 3g; Protein: 2g

Cinnamon Oranges

Serves 4 / Prep time: 10 minutes

Sweet, light, easy to prepare and nutritious, this simple dessert works any time of the year. Vitamin C–rich oranges are livened up with cinnamon and citrus juices to enhance the natural juiciness of orange. This dessert works well paired with French toast or with a topping of low-fat vanilla Greek yogurt.

4 navel oranges

2 tablespoons orange juice

2 tablespoons lemon juice

1 tablespoon sugar

½ teaspoon ground cinnamon

½ cup fresh raspberries

4 sprigs fresh mint

1. Using a sharp knife, remove the rind and white pith from the oranges. Cut each orange into 5 or 6 segments and arrange on 4 plates.

2. Whisk together the orange and lemon juices, sugar, and cinnamon, and spoon the mixture over the orange slices.

3. Top each serving with several raspberries and a sprig of fresh mint. Serve immediately.

Tip: The flavors of this recipe will be at their best in the winter when oranges are at their peak.

Storage: Store in an airtight container in the refrigerator for up to 1 day.

PER SERVING Calories: 90; Total Fat 0g; Saturated Fat: 0g; Cholesterol: 0mg; Sodium: 2mg; Potassium: 0mg; Total Carbohydrate: 20g; Fiber: 4g; Protein: 1g

Lemon Thins

Makes 30 cookies / Prep time: 15 minutes / Cook time: 8 to 10 minutes

Light, lemony, and healthy, this quick and easy recipe for lemon cookies is a perfect accompaniment to afternoon tea. These low-fat and low-sodium cookies use whole wheat pastry flour for added fiber and nutrition, and they get their zippy flavor from lemon zest.

Cooking spray

1 ¼ cups whole wheat pastry flour

⅓ cup cornstarch

1 ½ teaspoons baking powder

¾ cup sugar, divided

2 tablespoons butter, softened

2 tablespoons extra-virgin olive oil

1 large egg white

3 teaspoons freshly grated lemon zest

1 ½ teaspoons vanilla extract

4 tablespoons freshly squeezed lemon juice

1. Preheat the oven to 350°F. Coat two baking sheets with cooking spray.

2. In a mixing bowl, whisk together the flour, cornstarch, and baking powder.

3. In another mixing bowl beat ½ cup of the sugar, the butter, and olive oil with an electric mixer on medium speed until fluffy.

4. Add the egg white, lemon zest, and vanilla and beat until smooth. Beat in the lemon juice.

5. Add the dry ingredients to the wet ingredients and fold in with a rubber spatula just until combined.

6. Drop the dough by the teaspoonful, 2 inches apart, onto the prepared baking sheets.

7. Place the remaining ¼ cup sugar in a saucer. Coat the bottom of a wide-bottomed glass with cooking spray and dip it in the sugar. Flatten the dough with the glass bottom into 2 ½-inch circles, dipping the glass in the sugar each time.

8. Bake the cookies until they are just starting to brown around the edges, 8 to 10 minutes. Transfer to a flat surface (not a rack) to crisp.

Tip: You can substitute all-purpose flour for the whole wheat pastry flour.

Storage: Store in an airtight container for up to 3 days.

PER SERVING (1 cookie) Calories: 40; Total Fat 2g; Saturated Fat: 1g; Cholesterol: 2mg; Sodium: 26mg; Potassium: 3mg; Total Carbohydrate: 5g; Fiber: 1g; Protein: 1g

Banana Ice Cream

Serves 2 / Prep time: 3 to 5 minutes

SODIUM

LOWEST

MEATLESS
DAIRY-FREE
GLUTEN-FREE
LOW-FAT
ONE-POT

This super-easy, creamy, sweet, and cool dessert is free of added sugars, oil, and sodium and full of heart-healthy potassium. Using just one main ingredient, this delicious and healthy "ice cream" contains no dairy, takes minutes to make, and doesn't require an ice cream maker.

2 ripe bananas, sliced and frozen

OPTIONAL ADD-INS

Soy milk (or other milk)

Nuts

Nut butters

Honey

Fresh or dried fruit

Spices (cinnamon, mint, cardamom, ginger)

Cocoa

1. Add the frozen bananas and any desired additions to the bowl of a food processor and blend.

2. Occasionally scrape down the sides and continue to blend until smooth, approximately 3 to 5 minutes.

3. Scoop into 2 serving bowls and enjoy immediately as a soft serve. For firmer ice cream, place in an airtight, freezer-safe container and freeze for at least 1 hour.

Tip: Keep some peeled and sliced bananas in your freezer so they are available whenever you want to make the ice cream. Double or triple the batch and experiment with your favorite add-ins.

Storage: Store in individual-portion-size freezer-safe airtight containers for 2 to 3 months.

PER SERVING Calories: 122; Total Fat 0g; Saturated Fat: 0g; Cholesterol: 0mg; Sodium: 2mg; Potassium: 487mg; Total Carbohydrate: 31g; Fiber: 4g; Protein: 2g

Banana Cream Pie

Serves: 8 / Prep time: 10 minutes
Bake time: 5 minutes, plus 6 hours to overnight cooling time

This pie reminds me of many lakeside summer picnics. My Aunt Faye would use Jell-O and a graham cracker crust. Though not made from scratch, I could always taste the love.

3 cups whole milk

¾ cup white sugar

⅓ cup all-purpose flour

3 egg yolks, slightly beaten,
   or Egg Beaters

2 tablespoons unsalted butter

1 teaspoon vanilla

3 bananas

1 (9-inch) prebaked pie crust

1. In a large saucepan, scald the milk.

2. In another large saucepan, combine the sugar and flour. Over medium heat, gradually stir in the scalded milk, stirring constantly, and cook until thickened.

3. Cover and cook for 2 minutes more, stirring occasionally.

4. Stir ¼ cup of the hot sugar-milk mixture into the beaten egg yolks. When thoroughly combined, stir the yolk mixture into the remaining sugar-milk mixture. Cook for 1 minute more, stirring constantly.

5. Remove from the heat and blend in the butter and vanilla. Let the pie sit until it's cool.

6. When cool, slice the bananas and scatter on the pie crust. Pour the lukewarm sugar-milk mixture over the bananas. Wait until the pie is cool before serving, or refrigerate overnight for at least 6 hours.

PER SERVING Calories: 333; Total Fat 13g; Saturated Fat: 6g; Cholesterol: 88mg; Sodium: 151mg; Potassium: 342mg; Total Carbohydrate: 49g; Fiber: 2g; Protein: 6g

Snickerdoodle Chickpea Blondies

Serves 15 / Prep time: 10 minutes / Cook time: 30 to 35 minutes

This creative and healthy recipe for snickerdoodle blondies uses canned chickpeas to provide the perfect balance of starchiness, protein, and bulk in place of higher calorie and higher fat ingredients like milk, cream, oil, and eggs. Sweet and delicious, this guilt-free recipe is sure to become a favorite.

1 (15-ounce) can chickpeas, drained and rinsed

3 tablespoons nut butter of choice

¾ teaspoon baking powder

2 teaspoons vanilla extract

⅛ teaspoon baking soda

¾ cup brown sugar

1 tablespoon unsweetened applesauce

¼ cup ground flaxseed meal

2¼ teaspoons cinnamon

1. Preheat the oven to 350°F. Grease an 8-by-8-inch baking pan.

2. Blend all ingredients in a food processor until very smooth. Scoop into the prepared baking pan.

3. Bake until the tops are medium golden brown, 30 to 35 minutes. Allow the brownies to cool completely before cutting.

Tip: You can substitute an equal amount of quick oats for the flaxseed meal.

Storage: Store in an airtight container in the refrigerator for 3 to 4 days. You can also freeze the blondies by wrapping tightly in foil or plastic wrap and placing in heavy-duty freezer bags. Use within 1 to 2 months.

PER SERVING Calories: 85; Total Fat 2g; Saturated Fat: 0g; Cholesterol: 0mg; Sodium: 7mg; Potassium: 62mg; Total Carbohydrate: 16g; Fiber: 2g; Protein: 3g

Chocolate Chia Seed Pudding

Serves 4 / Prep time: 15 minutes, plus 3 to 5 hours or overnight to rest

This delicious, simple recipe for chocolate chia seed pudding is thick and creamy, and packed with protein and heart-healthy omega-3 fatty acids. Chia seeds can be found just about anywhere. With just 5 minutes preparation time, this pudding is perfect for a snack or dessert.

1 ½ cups unsweetened vanilla almond milk

¼ cup unsweetened cocoa powder

¼ cup maple syrup (or substitute any sweetener)

½ teaspoon vanilla extract

⅓ cup chia seeds

½ cup strawberries

¼ cup blueberries

¼ cup raspberries

2 tablespoons unsweetened coconut flakes

¼ to ½ teaspoon ground cinnamon (optional)

1. Add the almond milk, cocoa powder, maple syrup, and vanilla extract to a blender and blend until smooth. Whisk in chia seeds.

2. In a small bowl, gently mash the strawberries with a fork. Distribute the strawberry mash evenly to the bottom of 4 glass jars.

3. Pour equal portions of the blended milk-cocoa mixture into each of the jars and let the pudding rest in the refrigerator until it achieves a pudding like consistency, at least 3 to 5 hours and up to overnight.

4. Portion into serving bowls and top with blueberries, raspberries, coconut flakes, and cinnamon (if using).

Tip: You can also make this pudding without using a blender. Simply whisk the milk, cocoa and sweetener together until combined. Next add the chia seeds and mix again.

Storage: Leftovers can be stored in the refrigerator in an airtight container for 2 to 3 days, although the taste is best when it is fresh.

PER SERVING Calories: 189; Total Fat 7g; Saturated Fat: 2g; Cholesterol: 0mg; Sodium: 60mg; Potassium: 232mg; Total Carbohydrate: 28g; Fiber: 10g; Protein: 6g

Chocolate-Mint Truffles

Makes 60 small truffles / Prep time: 45 minutes / Bake time: 5 hours

MEATLESS
GLUTEN-FREE
LOW-FAT

Both decadent and low sodium, both the young and old enjoy these mint truffles in my house. The make a great accompaniment to afternoon tea or a sweet after-dinner treat.

14 ounces semisweet chocolate,
   coarsely chopped
¾ cup half-and-half
½ teaspoon pure vanilla extract
1½ teaspoon peppermint extract

2 tablespoons unsalted
   butter, softened
¾ cup naturally unsweetened or
   Dutch-process cocoa powder

1. Place semisweet chocolate in a large heatproof bowl.

2. Microwave in four 15-second increments, stirring after each, for a total of 60 seconds. Stir until almost completely melted. Set aside.

3. In a small saucepan over medium heat, heat the half-and-half, whisking occasionally, until it just begins to boil. Remove from the heat, then whisk in the vanilla and peppermint extracts.

4. Pour the mixture over the chocolate and, using a wooden spoon, gently stir in one direction.

5. Once the chocolate and cream are smooth, stir in the butter until it is combined and melted.

6. Cover with plastic wrap pressed on the top of the mixture, then let it sit at room temperature for 30 minutes.

7. After 30 minutes, place the mixture in the refrigerator until it is thick and can hold a ball shape, about 5 hours.

8. Line a large baking sheet with parchment paper or a use a silicone baking mat. Set aside.

9. Remove the mixture from the refrigerator. Place the cocoa powder in a bowl.

10. Scoop 1 teaspoon of the ganache and, using your hands, roll into a ball. Roll the ball in the cocoa powder, the place on the prepared baking sheet. (You can coat your palms with a little cocoa powder to prevent sticking).

11. Serve immediately or cover and store at room temperature for up to 1 week.

Tip: Layer truffles between parchment paper in a plastic storage container and store at room temperature or in the refrigerator for up to 1 week. Freeze for up to 2 months, then thaw overnight in the refrigerator.

PER SERVING Calories: 21; Total Fat 2g; Saturated Fat: 1g; Cholesterol: 2mg; Sodium: 2mg; Potassium: 21mg; Total Carbohydrate: 2g; Fiber: 1g; Protein: 0g

Personal Mango Pies

Serves 12 / Prep time: 15 minutes / Cook time: 14 to 16 minutes

These little mini pies are quick and easy to make and much healthier than a slice of pie. They are so low in calories and sodium you can have two at a time. Vitamin C and fiber-rich mango is used here, but peaches and apples also work well, so swap them out to make your favorite mini pies.

Cooking spray

12 small wonton wrappers

1 tablespoon cornstarch

½ cup water

3 cups finely chopped mango
 (fresh, or thawed from frozen,
 no sugar added)

2 tablespoons brown sugar
 (not packed)

½ teaspoon cinnamon

1 tablespoon light whipped butter
 or buttery spread

Unsweetened coconut flakes
 (optional)

1. Preheat the oven to 350°F.

2. Spray a 12-cup muffin pan with nonstick cooking spray.

3. Place a wonton wrapper into each cup of the muffin pan, pressing it into the bottom and up along the sides.

4. Lightly spray the wrappers with nonstick spray. Bake until lightly browned, about 8 minutes.

5. Meanwhile, in a medium nonstick saucepan, combine the cornstarch with the water and stir to dissolve. Add the mango, brown sugar, and cinnamon and turn heat to medium.

6. Stirring frequently, cook until the mangoes have slightly softened and the mixture is thick and gooey, 6 to 8 minutes.

7. Remove the mango mixture from heat and stir in the butter.

8. Spoon the mango mixture into wonton cups, about 3 tablespoons each. Top with coconut flakes (if using) and serve warm.

Tip: Wonton wrappers are stocked with the tofu in the refrigerated section of the supermarket.

Storage: If you are not serving all of these the same day they are made, don't add the filling to the wonton cups. Store the cups at room temperature in a sealed container or bag. Store the filling in the refrigerator in an airtight container and fill the cups right before serving. The filling will last up to 1 week in the refrigerator.

PER SERVING Calories: 61; Total Fat 1g; Saturated Fat: 0g; Cholesterol: 2mg; Sodium: 52mg; Potassium: 77mg; Total Carbohydrate: 14g; Fiber: 1g; Protein: 1g

RESOURCES

Healthy Eats

"What Fruits & Vegetables Are in Season?" Fruits and Veggies More Matters. Accessed 25 April, 2017. www.fruitsandveggiesmorematters.org /what-fruits-and-vegetables-are-in-season.

Marsha McCulloch. "Best Pantry Picks for a Low-Sodium Diet" Better Homes and Gardens. Accessed 24 April, 2017. www.bhg.com/recipes/healthy /low-sodium/best-low-sodium-pantry-picks/.

Food Safety and Inspection Service, United States Department of Agriculture. www.fsis.usda.gov/.

Food Network Healthy Eats (blog). http://blog.foodnetwork.com/healthyeats/.

Recipe Blogs

Organized Yourself Skinny (blog). www.organizeyourselfskinny.com.

All Recipes. www.allrecipes.com.

Heart Information

National Heart, Lung, and Blood Institute. www.nhlbi.nih.gov

The DASH Diet Eating Plan. www.dashdiet.org

American Heart Association. "Why High Blood Pressure is a 'Silent Killer.'" Accessed April 26, 2017. www.heart.org/HEARTORG/Conditions /HighBloodPressure/UnderstandSymptomsRisks/Why-High-Blood -Pressure-is-a-Silent-Killer_UCM_002053_Article.jsp#.WLXcPI-cFPY.

Harvard Medical School. "Heart failure and potassium." Accessed April 26, 2017. www.health.harvard.edu/heart-health/heart-failure-and-potassium.

REFERENCES

AllRecipes. "Brazilian Grilled Pineapple." Accessed May 11, 2017.
www.allrecipes.com/recipe/235932/brazilian-grilled-pineapple/.

American Heart Association. "Why High Blood Pressure is a 'Silent Killer.'"
Accessed May 11, 2017. www.heart.org/HEARTORG/Conditions
/HighBloodPressure/UnderstandSymptomsRisks/Why-High-Blood
-Pressure-is-a-Silent-Killer_UCM_002053_Article.jsp#.WLXcPI-cFPY.

The DASH Diet and Eating Plan. "What is the DASH Diet?" Accessed May 11,
2017. www.dashdiet.org/what_is_the_dash_diet.asp.

Diet and Fitness Today. "Potassium Rich Herbs and Spices." Accessed
May 11, 2017. www.dietandfitnesstoday.com/nutritionsorted.php?catid
=0200&nutid=306.

Fruits and Veggies—More Matters. "What Fruits & Vegetables Are in Season?"
Accessed April 25, 2017. www.fruitsandveggiesmorematters.org
/what-fruits-and-vegetables-are-in-season.

Harvard Health Publications: Harvard Medical School. "Heart Failure and
Potassium." Accessed April 26, 2017. www.health.harvard.ed/heart-health
/heart-failure-and-potassium.

Healthy Eats (blog). *Food Network*. Accessed May 11, 2017. blog.foodnetwork
.com/healthyeats/

Kresge, Tammy. "Chocolate and Peanut Butter Overnight Oats." *Organize
Yourself Skinny* (blog). Accessed May 11, 2017. www.organizeyourself
skinny.com/2014/06/15/peanut-butter-and-chocolate-overnight-oats/.

Mayo Clinic. "Sodium: How to Tame Your Salt Habit." Accessed May 11, 2017.
www.mayoclinic.org/healthy-lifestyle/nutrition-and-healthy-eating
/in-depth/sodium/art-20045479.

McCulloch, Marsha. "Best Pantry Picks for a Low-Sodium Diet." *Better Homes and Gardens*. Accessed April 24, 2017. www.bhg.com/recipes/healthy /low-sodium/best-low-sodium-pantry-picks/.

U.S. Department of Agriculture Food Safety and Inspection Service. Accessed May 11, 2017. www.fsis.usda.gov/.

U.S. Food and Drug Administration. "Guidance for Industry: A Food Labeling Guide (8. Claims)." Accessed May 11, 2017. www.fda.gov/Food /GuidanceRegulation/GuidanceDocumentsRegulatoryInformation /LabelingNutrition/ucm064908.htm

APPENDIX A
MEASUREMENT CONVERSIONS

Volume Equivalents (Dry)

US STANDARD	METRIC (APPROXIMATE)
⅛ teaspoon	0.5 mL
¼ teaspoon	1 mL
½ teaspoon	2 mL
¾ teaspoon	4 mL
1 teaspoon	5 mL
1 tablespoon	15 mL
¼ cup	59 mL
⅓ cup	79 mL
½ cup	118 mL
⅔ cup	156 mL
¾ cup	177 mL
1 cup	235 mL
2 cups or 1 pint	475 mL
3 cups	700 mL
4 cups or 1 quart	1 L
½ gallon	2 L
1 gallon	4 L

Volume Equivalents (Liquid)

US STANDARD	US STANDARD (OUNCES)	METRIC (APPROXIMATE)
2 tablespoons	1 fl. oz.	30 mL
¼ cup	2 fl. oz.	60 mL
½ cup	4 fl. oz.	120 mL
1 cup	8 fl. oz.	240 mL
1½ cups	12 fl. oz.	355 mL
2 cups or 1 pint	16 fl. oz.	475 mL
4 cups or 1 quart	32 fl. oz.	1 L
1 gallon	128 fl. oz.	4 L

Oven Temperatures

FAHRENHEIT (F)	CELSIUS (C) (APPROXIMATE)
250°F	120°C
300°F	150°C
325°F	165°C
350°F	180°C
375°F	190°C
400°F	200°C
425°F	220°C
450°F	230°C

Weight Equivalents

US STANDARD	METRIC (APPROXIMATE)
½ ounce	15 g
1 ounce	30 g
2 ounces	60 g
4 ounces	115 g
8 ounces	225 g
12 ounces	340 g
16 ounces or 1 pound	455 g

THE DIRTY DOZEN AND THE CLEAN FIFTEEN

A nonprofit and environmental watchdog organization called Environmental Working Group (EWG) looks at data supplied by the US Department of Agriculture (USDA) and the Food and Drug Administration (FDA) about pesticide residues and compiles a list each year of the best and worst pesticide loads found in commercial crops. You can refer to the Dirty Dozen list to know which fruits and vegetables you should always buy organic. The Clean Fifteen list lets you know which produce is considered safe enough when grown conventionally to allow you to skip the organics. This does not mean that the Clean Fifteen produce is pesticide-free, though, so wash these fruits and vegetables thoroughly.

These lists change every year, so make sure you look up the most recent before you fill your shopping cart. You'll find the most recent lists as well as a guide to pesticides in produce at EWG.org/FoodNews.

2017 Dirty Dozen

Apples
Celery
Cherry tomatoes
Cucumbers
Grapes
Nectarines
Peaches
Potatoes
Snap peas
Spinach
Strawberries
Sweet bell peppers

In addition to the Dirty Dozen, the EWG added two foods contaminated with highly toxic organophosphate insecticides:

Hot peppers
Kale/Collard greens

2017 Clean Fifteen

Asparagus
Avocados
Cabbage
Cantaloupe
Cauliflower
Eggplant
Grapefruit
Kiwis
Mangoes
Onions
Papayas
Pineapples
Sweet corn
Sweet peas (frozen)
Sweet potatoes

RECIPE INDEX

INDEX

ABOUT THE AUTHOR

In 2002, **CHRISTOPHER LOWER** caught a virus while traveling and wound up with an infection that settled into the enzymes in the fluid that surround his heart, causing the heart muscle tissue to inflame and enlarge. That began his heart health journey, which included several medications, a pacemaker, defibrillator, an LVAD (Left Ventricular Assist Device), and led to a heart transplant in May of 2014.

Though he was never a fan of diets, Christopher realized that if he was going to succeed with his new heart, he needed to change his lifestyle. Never one to turn down a challenge, he found a way to eat the foods he wanted and keep them healthy. You can follow Christopher's low sodium journey at HackingSalt.com.

CPSIA information can be obtained
at www.ICGtesting.com
Printed in the USA
BVOW10s1808200817
492373BV00003B/3/P